145 MPH

STORIES OF RISK-TAKING, ENTREPRENEURSHIP & INTEGRITY

JOHN MINNIHAN

Editor: Jennifer Penney
Indexer: John Minnihan
Cover Design: John Minnihan
Cover Photograph: Indian Chief Classic, Highway 50 near Hinckley, UT

For Jennifer, Blair and Brandon

Contents

Part IV: Corporate Life to Entrepreneur: Flipping the Switch   67

Part V: Entrepreneurial Risk-taking After a Failure   83

Part VI: The Entrepreneur As Family Man   115

PREFACE

Common themes have emerged at inflection points in my life. When I started paying attention to this, I realized how much my decision-making, personal character and choices today are impacted by my earliest encounters with risk-taking.

I wrote this book to explore the nexus of risk-taking, entrepreneurship and integrity.

These were life changing moments that weren't entirely obvious as they were occurring. I hope you enjoy reading about this and that it helps you identify the patterns in your own life that influence your decisions.

PART I: EARLY RISK-TAKING

RISK VS. REWARD: CHILDHOOD DARES & ADRENALINE RUSH

Sometime in the second or third grade I discovered the adrenaline rush. It was mysterious & pleasing - unlike anything I'd experienced before - and I quickly learned that I could make it happen at will. By doing scary, daring things.

So I did those things. A lot.

The first dare-devilish thing I recall doing was climbing onto the roof of the picnic structure in the park across the street from our house. It wasn't huge or necessarily very high off the ground, perhaps 12 - 14 feet at its highest point in the middle.

It was a poured concrete roof, made in sections that were positioned at moderate angles to each other, resembling a giant folded piece of origami set upon a collection of steel poles at each corner and another that bisected the roof on each side.

The roof itself was unspectacular - its importance lay solely in that it could be climbed, not entirely easily, but with effort anyone could get onto it. Of course, not just anyone did. In fact, almost no one did. I did, as did my brothers and a few friends.

Almost immediately, we discovered that it if we were seen on the roof by the park workers or the police who occasionally patrolled the park, we'd get into trouble. One of my brothers' friends had been caught on the roof & had to have his parents come pick him up at the police station.

Even though he'd seen the police coming down the park service road, he mistakenly believed that he couldn't be seen. So he stayed on the roof & was easily caught.

I overheard this story told to my brothers, but didn't think much of it until the next time I was in the park on the roof. A police car came down the service road and I was convinced that if I was caught, I'd be taken to jail. I didn't want to go to jail.

Recall I was in the third grade & didn't have a fully formed concept of what would have happened "in jail", so I ran across the top of the roof to the other side & jumped off into the grass below.

This was a jump of perhaps 8 to 9 vertical feet with a lateral distance across another 10 feet. I was surprised that I wasn't hurt & took off running.

The feeling I got - that adrenaline rush from jumping off the roof - was intense. I wanted to experience that again, so I began to go into the park for the sole purpose of climbing that picnic structure and jumping off.

I also climbed & jumped from the park's bathroom building and virtually every piece of play equipment that was climbable. This was a great feeling & I could control exactly when & where I experienced it.

Over the next few years, I'd perform progressively more dangerous stunts on my bicycle, such as riding as fast as I could down the hill & jumping over the creek, a la Evel Knievel. This would foreshadow my later fascination with motorcycle jumps by several years.

During this period, I learned to manage my risk to reward ratio pretty well. I didn't realize I was doing this, of course, nor did I have a name for it. I did, however, spend time judging how far I jump safely, how far I had to jump to get a rush, and determining exactly how close to the 'safe' line I could get without going over.

This served me well until I was 10 when I got a new Spider bicycle with a banana seat. I rode that bike everywhere - in the park, around the neighborhood and to school.

I was hot shit. I loved that bike & felt like I could go anywhere. So I did, at least, in my mind.

LEARNING TO JUMP

That Spider was the first new bike I'd had - every other one was a hand-me-down from my older brothers, or something that my parents had purchased used.

I absolutely loved that bike. It was a Schwinn Stingray - the type with the chopper-style handlebars and a banana-shaped seat. It was fantastic and I felt great riding it; it simply glided along almost effortlessly.

I quickly began riding my bike outside the neighborhood, first going to my school, which was about a mile away, and then further beyond it. Soon, I was riding as much as five or six miles from home. The freedom that bike provided was enormous.

Though it took me greater distances from home, I experienced the greatest influence that bike would have on my life in that same park across the street from my house.

I learned to **jump**.

The park was essentially a giant bowl, not unlike the type you find in ski areas, only smaller. It was bounded by large hills on each side, both sloping downward in the center to a creek that bisected the park.

The creek usually had water in it and the terrain was such that the creek itself had a distinct "cut", easily twenty five - thirty feet deep, sharply turned from the somewhat flat bottom land where the bounding hills of the park met. This created an excellent set of natural ramps for bicycle jumps.

It was here I learned how to jump. Racing down the park hill, sometimes starting in my own driveway and speeding across the street onto the park service road, continuing to pedal as fast as I could until the bike was moving faster than I was pedaling. I would bound down into the creek itself, occasionally crashing, but jumping successfully often enough that I was hooked.

I'd sometimes do this for hours and would repeat this type of relentless practice years later on my Wombat[1].

_____

[1] Hodaka Wombat off-road motorcycle, sometimes referred to a Combat Wombat

GOING MOBILE: A SCOOTER AT 9 AND MOTORCYCLE AT 12

My dad bought a Cushman Scooter when I was nine years old. As far as I can recall, this was just a toy for him.

This bike had a tractor-style saddle seat, side bags and two-speed transmission with a shifter that extended nearly three feet up alongside the engine. The windshield was two-tone clear and red plastic and it had a lot of chrome.

The front wheel and tire were considerably smaller than the back and it had a pretty small gas tank. This scooter was meant to be ridden in parades by a guy with a funny red hat.

This was the first 'motorcycle' that I rode. We'd take turns riding it up and down our neighborhood street, turning around at the end of the block.

It didn't go fast by any stretch of the imagination, but it had a throttle and would accelerate when it was turned. Though it spent a lot of time in the garage, when we did get it out, it was a blast.

I was hooked on motos[2].

My oldest brother got a motorcycle when he was 15. I don't recall whether my parents bought it or he bought it himself. It was a Kawasaki 100cc, the sort that was a cross between a trail bike & a street bike. It was nothing special, really, but there it was - in the garage.

---

[2] Motos, short for motorcycles

I was allowed to ride it in the backyard, essentially in circles around the perimeter of our 1/2 acre lot. That must have thrilled the neighbors - it was not a quiet bike.

I rode it in the yard as much as I could, but my brother didn't ride it very much at all.   I recall initially being disappointed by that ("why isn't he riding this perfectly good motorcycle?"), but quickly realized that he was simply no longer interested in it after he got his driver's license - the car was now his focus.

So the bike stayed in the garage for weeks gathering dust. One day when no one else was home, I rode it around the yard for a few minutes before deciding to go riding on the street. I don't recall particulars, but there was a 1 - 2 hour period each weekday when I was the only one home.

I used this time to ride the motorcycle further & further from home. I discovered a set of trails several miles from home that I could reach by riding the bike along a foot path that we used to walk to neighborhoods that would have otherwise required a long drive in a car.

I learned how to ride the bike on dirt trails & began to experiment with some jumps. The techniques I'd developed on my bicycle over the past couple years were surprisingly relevant; with just a little tweaking, I was jumping pretty well.

I kept riding the 100 like that for at least a couple years, going further and further from home and spending hours a week on it. When I was 14, my other brother got his own motorcycle - a

Yamaha 500. This was a real bike. It was totally badass: purple, loud and fast.

I began sneaking the 500 out almost immediately. It was on this bike that I first went somewhat fast, just over 75mph.

I'd ride the 500 any chance I got. My brother had an after-school job & he'd simply drive his car, a VW Bug, straight from school to his job each day. That left me lots of time to ride the 500.

One day, against all odds, I encountered my brother at a stoplight while I was out riding. Across four lanes of traffic on the opposite side, I saw his truck (he'd bought a pickup truck as well) & him at the wheel. There was nothing I could do, so I behaved as casually as I could and slowly pulled away when the light changed. We passed each other with two lanes of cars between us and I did not look over at him.

Convinced I was busted, I cut through the neighborhoods and back-tracked home as quickly as possible. I learned later that he had indeed come home to check on whether his bike had been stolen; seeing it in the garage, he simply went back to work.

He didn't know that I'd parked it probably less than two minutes earlier and had run across the back yard to my friend's house. This was a near miss that wouldn't repeat itself six months later when he caught me & that same friend out driving his Bug[3].

---

[3] Volkswagen Beetle, often referred to as a Bug

A FAST CAR: THIS CHANGES EVERYTHING

When I was 15, my dad did something extraordinary: he bought me a car. This was extraordinary for two reasons: I was a year from being able to legally drive and the car was a 1968 Camaro, a car that I'd decided had to be my first car because Mannix[4] drove one.

I turned 16 and got my license that day. Perhaps a harbinger of things to come, I got two tickets that day: for speeding & careless driving. I was - surprise - speeding down my street to the corner, turning into it in the way that's today known as drifting - we called it fish-tailing then - and the back end of my car nearly clipped a police car as I glided around the corner at 50+ mph. Whoops.

But it didn't matter. I was cool, far cooler than any of my friends: I had a car. Not just any car, either, but a '68 Camaro. I loved that car. But it wasn't fast enough; it had a straight-six 230ci engine that I hated.

I was determined to build a race car and learned everything I could about performance tuning that six cylinder. I came across a company called Peterson Engineering, I think, in the back of a hot rod magazine, that offered some kind of kit for the 230. I didn't buy it, but did use some tricks I read about to adjust the jets (maybe singular 'jet', I don't recall) on the carb to slightly increase

---

[4] Joe Mannix, a fictional detective in a television series that aired from 1967 - 1975. Mannix actually drove a 1968 Dodge Dart convertible in the second season. They look a bit similar, but I would not today confuse a Dart with a Camaro. I'm baffled as to how I made this mistake back then, as I turned 15 in 1977 only two years after the series ended.

performance. I replaced the stock muffler with a Thrush and convinced myself that it now had more horsepower.

The car sounded great, looked great and was a blast to drive. I began working on the body, preparing to paint it. I spent a few months sanding it, repairing the rust that had accumulated just under the fender-wells, and even installed a Z28 spoiler on the trunk lid.

Around this time, my family moved out to the rural area near Six Flags[5], just outside St. Louis. This was somewhat disruptive for me, as I had close friends back in my old neighborhood. But I now had a place to really work on my car, so I set up an outdoor mechanic's bay under a large oak tree.

I wasn't just working on my car during this time, though - I was deciding what I wanted to with my life. I was becoming increasingly less interested in performing at school; the unusually high scores I'd made on pretty much every standardized test since 3rd grade meant that I was in 'advanced this' and 'college prep that' classes.

In my sophomore year, I began purposely bombing the new tests I'd be given, finally stating 'no more'. I didn't really want to attend another year at my current high school, and in fact was seriously considering quitting to focus on becoming a stunt man.

I rode out my junior year with no particular issues beyond having been banned from driving to school the first week. I'd been doing donuts in the parking lot when the assistant principal,

---

[5] Six Flags Amusement Park

who looked like WC Fields after a three day bender, came running toward my car yelling "Stop!"

Or so I'm told. I neither saw nor heard him till it was too late. I just missed hitting him while accelerating out of a donut, throwing burning tire smoke into the air like a pro, going perhaps 45mph. It wasn't all that fast, but he had to jump out of the way to avoid being struck.

He's the same assistant principal who'd been afraid to suspend my brother when he rode his motorcycle (the 500 I used to 'borrow') inside the high school, while he & half a dozen staff members watched.

So I lost my parking privilege, which in practical terms, meant I could no longer drive to school. I briefly considered just ignoring the ban, but he threatened to have my car towed & I decided I didn't need the hassle.

So though it was disruptive to my friendships, the move did come at a great time. I avoided quitting school, opting instead to see what the new high school was like. It was my senior year and I was determined to have some fun.

As I explore in depth later, I meant Jim almost immediately. Jim had a reputation for being wild, but not in a threatening way. He was just pretty weird - wearing a helmet when he drove his car, stuff like that.

We complimented each other's personalities pretty well. People at school quickly came to believe that I was crazy - I have no idea where this came from, but it emerged almost immediately. So I worked with it.

I'd go to parties and see some of the jocks giving a guy shit. This is the kind of stuff where when I'd seen it before, I'd intervened. What was different this time is that these new guys were actually afraid - it was fascinating & created a new sense of power.

On this one occasion early in the school year, we were all at a party when one of the jocks, a popular guy who I'd met & had no issues with, took another guy's hat & wouldn't give it back.

The kid was desperate to get his hat back, but Jim (different Jim) wouldn't give it back. From where I as standing, it looked like the guy being teased (if I ever knew his name, I've long since forgotten it) was starting to cry.

That's when I went over to Jim & told him, plainly & slowly, "Give him back his hat." I stood inches from his face & repeated myself: "Give him back his hat."

I said nothing else, but continued to stare at Jim, now a bit further back and with my right arm slightly raised, elbow cocked and my fist into a shape I'd seen tae kwon do fighters use. I continued to stare at him, moving with him as he began to back away, never losing eye contact.

He finally said "Here's your hat..." and threw it back to the guy he'd been teasing, laughing nervously as if to ask me "are we done?" and so I began to back away.

I heard him say "You're f*cking crazy" as he walked away. Nah, I just don't tolerate bullies.

I worked on my car for hours a day. Using the area I'd setup under the tree, I swapped out the 230 for a 327 I bought from an acquaintance. I think he'd wrecked his Z28[6] and was now parting it out; I was happy to get the engine.

I later heard stories of how this may have been a 302, but I could never confirm that. In any case, it was only briefly in my Camaro, as it seized up one afternoon in my driveway and never ran again. The story of how that happened is worth telling.

The road up to my parent's house is long and windy, and more than once I sought a shortcut. One day, I realized that the creek running along the base of the mountain ran directly behind my parent's neighborhood, which was just a collection of 10 or 12 houses built in random spots along the top & back of the mountain.

Using the creek as a road cut at least 5 minutes of drive time off the ride. When the creek was dry, like it usually was, this was really no more complicated than driving on a bumpy gravel road. You had to slow down in some spots, because there were really large rocks that you had to drive around, or you'd get stuck.

Well, I bottomed out on one of those large rocks that I was trying to avoid. I heard it & I felt it, but I had no idea that I'd

---

[6] Camaro Z28, the Chevrolet model designator used to identify a specific engine & trim package. The Z28 had a higher-performance engine, a spoiler and painted race stripes.

punctured the oil pan. The engine was hot & so was the oil - it ran out of the pan like hot butter on the final 3/4 mile to my house.

I got as far as the bottom of the driveway before the engine seized. The block was cracked & so the 327, which may have been a rare 302, was toast.

I replaced it with a 350 and then later replaced the 350 with a 400. That 400, with a Turbo 350 transmission, 3200 rpm stall speed convertor, B&M Quicksilver[7] shifter and subframe connecting kit was running perfectly when my brother drove it into a grove of trees.

I talk about that later.

---

[7] The Quicksilver provided manual shifting of an automatic transmission. This allowed the driver to deliver more torque to the drivetrain than automatic shifting.

Before we moved, I'd been best friends since 8th grade with the guy who lived directly behind me - his name was Russell. While most of our early time together was spent doing harmless stuff like riding our bikes at night, once Russ got his license in 10th grade, you could say that all hell broke loose.

And since you're wondering, I'll mention briefly that I went to a Catholic high school, Rosary, my freshman year and hated it. I'd made the decision myself, almost choosing to go to St.Louis University High (I'd been accepted) because I was convinced that it was the best way to get academically prepared for college. I expected to go to MIT or Stanford; I hadn't decided yet which one. I chose Rosary[8] because it had bus service to my neighborhood and wouldn't require over an hour of public transit each way, like SLUH would have.

I remember two things from my freshman year:

1. I hated the nuns. Most had no business being around other people, let alone teaching teenagers. Every argument I'd made with myself the previous year about getting a better education at a private Catholic school was vaporized by these backward relics from another century. On the plus side, it did cement in my mind the ridiculousness of organized religion.

2. One day I was walking up the street from the school, maybe to catch a late bus. I don't remember why I was there, but I was. And so was James (no last names). He was getting teased by

---

[8] Rosary Catholic High School, a private high school in Spanish Lake, Missouri

another student, who I recognized, but didn't really know. I could see that James was upset, but they were on the other side of the street and it looked like it was just some name-calling.

But then the bully started pushing James. I was incensed - I recall to this day how angry that made me. I picked up a large board, maybe a 2x4, that was on the side of the road, and ran across the street yelling at the bully to "Knock it off!" I don't think he took me seriously at first, because he didn't stop. I raised the board above & behind my head, choking it up like it was giant baseball bat. The bully's head was to be the ball. Startled, he ran off. I saw him at school several times after that & he always looked away quickly, never saying a word.

James thanked me, but he left the school within a few weeks of that incident & I have no idea where he went.

Anyway, I left Rosary, too. I didn't go back and instead went to McClure[9] for 10th grade. This put Russ & I together a lot, but in an ironic twist, he'd also switched schools - he was going to a vocational-technology school where he was learning diesel mechanics. He talked about getting a job working on tractor trailers or forklifts; to the best of my knowledge, he never got a job doing anything like that.

After school, though, we would get together and go driving around. During one of the driving trips, we discovered a road with a bridge that can be best described as insanely designed & haphazardly built. It went over a set of railroad tracks that had

---

[9] McClure Senior High School, a public high school in Ferguson, Missouri

been there for decades, with the surrounding neighborhoods growing up around (and in spite of) it.

The road itself, Dade Road, was built at nearly the exact same elevation as the railroad tracks. The neighborhood it went thru was old, and so had scores of houses built right to the railway right-of-way, which was about 40 feet wide on either side of the tracks. There was no room to build a proper bridge, but the amount of traffic that went across the tracks had grown to more than could be safely managed with an at-grade crossing.

So they built a bridge that abruptly and unnaturally raised the road to a height sufficient to allow trains to traverse beneath it and then just as abruptly pitched back down to the original road elevation on the other side.

It looked something like this:

without much exaggeration, either. This meant that under normal driving conditions, at the posted speed limit, a car crossing Dade Bridge would experience the equivalent of hitting a speed bump, briefly flatten out on the top of the bridge itself, and then "drop off" the other side.

Naturally, we saw it as a jump. So we jumped it, repeatedly. One particular evening, we hit the bridge at 65 mph. Keep in mind this was a 30 mph street and the bridge has a reduced speed limit of 20. Yeah, hitting it at 45mph over the speed limit was a great idea. We'd sat in his truck at the far end of Dade Road, estimating how fast we'd have to hit the bridge to come off the ground a little bit. We overestimated by at least a factor of two.

It was one of the few times I ever recall being scared by Russell's driving - when we hit the top of the first ramp on the bridge, we went airborne. We flew over the flat part of the bridge, hitting nose-first about half-way down the ramp on the other side. We both hit the ceiling and were mildly injured, in fact. That was the last time we jumped Dade Bridge, by the way.

This is the lesson I learned from Dade Bridge:

Estimate well or **die**.

This became incredibly important to me later when I began attempting more aggressive jumps on my motorcycle - it may have even saved my life.

PART II: FRIENDS – AND THINGS – FEED THE NEED

HOW FRIENDS ENABLE RISK-TAKING

As a teenager, both of my long-term best friends were risk-takers like me. This wasn't a conscious choice, per se, but it wasn't entirely random either.

Both Russell and Jim entered my life when they became my neighbors - Russell literally and Jim a bit more loosely. The connections that we developed centered around risk-taking. With Jim at least, some of his thrill-seeking seemed pathological, from my perspective as an adult.

In retrospect, I believe that I would have done fewer of these risky acts on my own, at least initially. That doesn't explain the solo motorcycle jumping, but it's impossible to know whether that would have emerged without these earlier adventures.

Everything builds from earlier experiences.

I fed their risk-taking and they fed mine.

Our friendships were in equilibrium in that regard.

Russell had a pickup that he wanted to race. He rebuilt the engine, painted it black and added some stripes, but it was still just a truck.

He tried to change that by removing the bed and putting slicks[10] on it. They may have actually been minimally-treaded street tires, but my recollection is these were slicks.

One night we were out driving around and he decided to do some burnouts. I spontaneously decided to sit on the exposed frame of the truck just above the rear axle as Russ began smoking the tires. I adjusted where I sat twice as my first two choices had no hand-holds and I nearly fell off. This was an experience that today is hard to describe; it was loud, visually alarming - full of black smoke - and smelled acrid with burning rubber.

It was a full sensory overload experience that was a huge adrenalin rush. In the midst of the burn-out, I could see nothing but the tire smoke. I could only hear the squealing of the tires, as they were melting on the road surface, and the engine as it screamed to higher and higher RPMs.

It was something that no one else had done.

This episode, while seemingly ridiculous, random and ill-advised, illustrates how my risk-taking began to follow specific patterns:

---

[10] Slicks are no-tread racing tires. These are treadless to place as much rubber surface area on the track as possible, increasing traction and reducing loss of usable torque.

I would **seize an opportunity** as it was presented.

I'd arrange for minimal safety - **risk mitigation** - in the moment, but no more.

And finally, I'd use these experiences to inform my future decisions, i.e. 'that wasn't so bad' or 'that was really, really bad', and **adjust my responses to new situations** accordingly.

THE HELMET-WEARING DATSUN DRIVER

The pale-yellow Datsun B210 swerved past the school bus out onto the grass, its horn honking as wildly as it was being driven.

"Who the hell is that?" I asked in mock interest to the girl sitting next me. "That's Jim", she said. I noticed another detail as the car sped away from my new high school. The driver – Jim – was wearing a helmet.

I learned later that day that Jim lived by me. My family & I had just moved from the northern St. Louis suburbs out to what seemed like the backwoods. Our new house was nice, but its location was far more attractive than the home itself: it sat atop one of the rolling hills in the area, and Jim lived down in the valley a couple miles away.

We quickly formed a friendship, mostly of convenience at first. We were both seniors and had an interest in cars; we owned a total of 22 between us.

My sister developed an immediate crush on Jim. Her crush was short-lived; our friendship grew. We began spending most days after school hanging out with each other, and occasionally other neighborhood guys. Jim and I became best friends quickly.

And we quickly got into some really crazy situations. As I grew older, I'd relish the opportunity to tell new friends about some of my adventures with Jim. Often, they wouldn't believe the stories because they were just too outrageous. One of these new friends even suggested that Jim was my alter ego; Jim didn't really exist, these stories were about me.

Years ago, I started writing a book of Jim Stories, but had doubts about its capacity to hold up as a complete work. That is, individual stories may be interesting and amazing, but as a whole the collection may not be compelling enough to sell well. I also had a genuine fear of people copying the stunts that would be retold in that book. The fact that Jim and I lived through them the first time is more likely attributable to dumb luck than skill. It certainly wasn't due to careful planning. But I digress.

One evening, we decided to climb the radio & television tower on the high mountain behind Greensfelder Park.

That involved climbing up and over a fence that surrounded the power station & equipment building at the base of the tower and then methodically climbing the lattice framework of the tower to the top.

I'm going to leave out some details that I feel are especially dangerous to recount, but trust me when I say that the climb was thrilling and the view from the top was amazing.

This tower climb exposed the beginnings of a divergence between Jim's risk-taking and my own. His seemed ever-more truly life-threatening - there was never a safety net or backup in case something went wrong.

I had no trouble accepting risk, but as I've mentioned already, I was developing a keen awareness that only I could - or should - accept risks for myself.

Being along for the ride when Jim took on enormous risks placed me in situations I wouldn't have chosen on my own.

More on that later.

Still, though: we both did this stuff anyway because it was such an immediate rush. This thing needed to be fed.

A TRASHCAN FULL OF SCHOLARSHIPS

This is a topic that's difficult for me to talk about now. I mentioned earlier that I did very well on the standardized tests that high schoolers typically take.

I did so well on one of the assessment tests that college solicitations began to arrive in the mail in high volume. Most days, there were at least two and some days nine or ten of these mailers were delivered:

"Come to our school!"
"We want you!"
etc.

A few of these included explicit offers of scholarships. Full payment of fees. Free college.

Along with all the others, I threw these in the trash. I discussed this with no one. Even though my parents must have had awareness of this as it was happening, neither of them mentioned it to me or even asked about it.

This is a decision that I regret in the abstract. Had I pursued any of those offers, my life would have taken a different direction. I wouldn't have ended up in Denver, nor would I have met and married Jennifer, nor had two amazing sons with her.

So I wouldn't trade, but I do wonder about the *what ifs* from time to time.

Jim and I had known each other for a few weeks and this was the first night we went out driving around together. He drove the same old Datsun I'd seen him in that first day of school. He'd been doing some bodywork on it, adding "ground effects"[11] panels made from street signs. These were riveted onto the original body, and now the whole car was primer gray. The interior was as non-stock as the body; he had a CB[12], a great stereo and the beginnings of a custom control panel full of switches for lights & horns.

Valley Park is about 15 miles from where we lived and is your typical, old river town that hadn't changed much since its heyday in the Fifties. One main street ran through town, where the little general store, gas station and feed store were. A lot of roads were dirt or gravel. It's considerably more modern now, of course.

We were driving around on the old dirt roads in the river bottoms, that big expanse of land that is flat and wide and floods out every time the river breaches its banks. There are hundreds of mature oaks & cottonwoods down there, with plenty of darkness this time of night and several unmarked railroad crossings.

Jim stopped the car at one of these crossings as a train was lumbering by slowly. What he did next was surprising.

---

[11] Ground effects are aerodynamic features added to a car's body or chassis to create downforce which in turn increases a car's grip, allowing for higher speed during cornering

[12] Citizens band radio

He jumped out of the car - leaving the engine running and the driver door wide open - and ran toward the train.

He turned and continued running alongside the train, almost at an even pace. As he neared the end of a box car, he reached out and grabbed hold of the exposed hand rail and hoisted himself onto the train.

I was already out of the car running alongside the train by this time, assessing the risk of jumping onto it. I hopped on and held onto the exterior of a car.

I saw Jim move from one car to the next at least twice until finally, I could no longer see him. I chose not to move to another car.

As the train picked up speed, I continued to assess and adjust my position on the car, looking out and ahead for a place to jump off, hoping to minimize injury. I briefly considered that if I didn't push-off as I jumped, I'd roll under the train and be killed. Push hard…

I twisted my ankle when I landed, but was otherwise uninjured after having ridden the train for less than a mile. I walked back to the car and waited for Jim.

I've thought a lot about the train episode over the years. There are parallels to starting and building a business.

—

You have to constantly **pay attention** to what is happening **right now** or you'll run out of operating capital - *fall off the train and get killed.*

But you also have to keep looking ahead and to the side - **planning and executing** - otherwise you'll be unprepared when that big customer abruptly changes course and doesn't sign the deal with you, or the fickle consumer market chooses the other player - *the train speeds up and you're stuck riding it for 30 miles until it slows down enough to jump off.*

You may be **tempted to copy everything that your competition is doing** - *Jim on the train, jumping from car to car* - but if you and your organization aren't prepared for it, you'll fail. *You'll fall off the train.*

The metaphors are plentiful. Pick virtually any business process and the train episode has an analog. It's eerily applicable to so many situations.

We'd been at the pool hall in Eureka[13] having a beer and playing a couple games. I don't recall how Russell, my brother Tom and I ended up there, as we didn't typically hang out together.

But we were there and I had driven. As we left the pool hall and approached my car, Tom asked me if he could drive. I'd only had one beer; that's all the spare cash I had on me that evening as I was also paying for the games. I think he said something about him having had less to drink than me, which in that moment might have made sense.

I let him drive.

He had no experience with any fast car and had never driven my Camaro. At that time, the car had a small block 400 that had come out of a 1970 Chevelle.

This particular engine was actually a 402 that produced 375 hp. In the Camaro, which was 630 pounds lighter than a Chevelle, this was a powerhouse. I also had a B&M Quicksilver ratchet shifter.

The Quicksilver allowed you to manually shift through the gears even though it was an automatic transmission. This meant that slam-shifting was easy to do and if the driver was skilled, they could get a few extra foot-pounds of torque out of each gear. This gave the Camaro a distinct hop as you shifted.

---

[13] Eureka, Missouri

That shifter almost got us all killed.

Tom was enthralled with the car's performance as we drove down the outer road that skirted the new part of Eureka. He progressively picked up speed and began playing with downshifting as we approached other cars.

We reached the stop sign (which is now a light) at the end of the outer road. As we pulled away from the stop and proceeded onto Fox Creek Road, Tom began to aggressively hold out the next shift, causing the car to wildly hop when he did shift.

Critically, it began to rain as we neared the end of the straight section of road, just before a sharp drop-off into a narrow mini-canyon that hugged the creek. This is also where the road abruptly turns inward toward the canyon wall.

We were doing approximately 100mph as we entered that turn. Tom tried to slow down by braking, but we began to slide as the rain had made the roadway incredibly slick. He downshifted, twice.

This caused the rear of the Camaro to wildly hop to the the left before the tires gained traction on the much dryer pavement that was under the 'tree tunnel' the road was now entering.

This shot us into the trees off the right side of the road at perhaps 90 mph. We hit several small trees before coming to a stop against a larger tree.

We all walked away from that wreck but it taught me a critical lesson.

—

Never allow someone else to commit you to a high-risk situation. The only person who can manage your risk profile is you.

I bought a Corvette that I didn't need, which is probably how every Corvette story begins.

It was red and fast. Showing up to Monsanto[14] as a coop student driving a new red Vette and wearing a sharkskin suit must have been quite a visual.

About this same time, Jim had somehow come into possession of a Porsche 911. I think he was supposed to be doing mechanical work of some sort on it, but he kept the car for a long time. And he drove it a lot.

We would rat race[15] from time to time - him in the 911 and me in the Vette - and this became a bit of a habit. Occasionally, we'd be out driving in the Vette and we'd do speed tests.

The Vette had a digital speedometer and there was a certain thrill to watching the numbers climb as the car picked up speed. They'd change rapidly at first and progressively slow as I reached very high speed.

134... 135... 136... 137

I got it up to 137 mph one night out on Highway 44 driving home. It was around 11pm and I had to work the next day, so I wanted to get home quickly to get some sleep.

---

[14] Monsanto Chemical Company in St. Louis, Missouri

[15] rat racing is a game of cat and mouse on the highway. one driver chases the other.

I passed exactly three cars in those 15 miles where I was traveling at high speed. Two of them had cell phones and called the police. This was ironic, as cell phones were still pretty rare in cars (though I had one in my Peugeot).

Anyway, the police received a report of a "…late model red Corvette traveling west-bound at a high rate of speed". One of the St. Louis County cops who heard the radio call responded with "that sounds like Minnihan".

I shit you not, my friends. I had one of the only new red Vettes in Eureka and was known to… drive fast.

Unbeknownst to me, two state patrol cars also picked up the call and were attempting to catch up to me on westbound 44. I never saw or heard them.

St. Louis County and Eureka police decided that if the red Vette was indeed me, I'd be getting off the highway at the Allenton[16] exit.

They setup a road block at the bottom of the exit ramp.

I'd slowed down to about 95mph as I exited the highway onto the over 1/4 mile long ramp that connected to Allenton Road. The spotlights were turned on immediately.

I slammed on the brakes and came to a stop well short of the multiple police cars that I could see. After assessing the situation,

---

[16] Allenton, Missouri. This little town was just west of Eureka.

I threw the car into reverse and began backing up the ramp with the intention of hopping back onto the highway. As one does.

I then saw the two highway patrol cars, lights and sirens blaring, speeding toward me. That was unexpected.

I stopped, drove forward a bit then stopped again. I got out of the car as the state patrol cars were pulling in sideways behind me to block my route back onto the highway.

I heard someone yell *"John?"*

I recognized the voice as that of a St. Louis County policeman named Don (or was it Doug?). I called back to him *"Is that you, Don?"*.

"Yeah, it's Don. Come on down here, John."

So I walked down to the road block where it was a mixture of a reunion with the cops who knew me and some angry cursing from those who didn't.

I got a couple tickets and Don was nice enough to drive the Vette over to the parking lot of the hotel at the corner, as they weren't going to let me drive again that night.

So anyway, Jim and I tended to drive fast.

One Sunday morning, we drove (the Vette only) into downtown St. Louis and discovered two things:

The streets were empty and the Vette made an insanely loud exhaust noise that echoed between the tall buildings as we sped from street to street.

We'd been doing this for a few minutes when I heard sirens. Convinced I was going to get yet another ticket for the hell-raising (it was *really, really* loud), I sped east out of the core downtown toward Highway 70.

We reached the last surface street before the highway ramp and I floored it. There was one last turn at the end of this street where it connected to the ramp.

I was going way too fast to make that corner. As I turned, the car fish-tailed around and I over-corrected, sending us off the ramp two or three feet off the ground.

We sailed over part of an empty lot on the other side and below the ramp, clipping a street sign and coming to rest in the dirt about a 120 feet or so later.

The front passenger tire was shredded and the wheel was bent. There was fiberglass damage in the cowl and quarter panel, but neither of us were injured.

I put the space-saver spare tire on and we drove home.

I got rid of the Vette not long after that.

—

I think the lesson here is **nobody** needs a Vette.

Jim had bought an old discarded fiberglass paddleboat that had been used in one of those small lakes that caters to tourists. The tourist would pay to rent the boat for 1/2 hour or an hour and paddle around the lake, using bicycle style foot pedals that drove paddles just below the water's surface.

When Jim got this boat, the paddles were long gone and the hole where the pedal system had been was patched. This was cracked, though, and so the boat was not seaworthy.

He was repairing that when he decided to attach a large outboard motor to the boat. This was either an Evinrude or Mercury - I think he had one of each around this time - 135hp engine.

This engine was way too heavy for the boat. It hadn't been designed to carry *any* engine, let alone one this heavy relative to the overall weight of the boat.

I didn't see much of the work he did to attach the engine, but recall the outcome with clarity: he attached a steel plate to the back of the boat using huge bolts, then attached the engine to the plate, and finally used marine epoxy to seal the bolt-holes.

And thus we had a 9 foot long fiberglass boat with seats molded into the shell, powered by a 135hp outboard designed for a vessel at least twice as big.

What could go wrong?

To my knowledge, the only time that boat was ever in the water was when we launched it out into the Illinois River one Sunday.

The day was overcast, windy and threatening rain. It was almost cold, in fact. I honestly can't recall how we got this ridiculous boat out to the river, but another Jim (yeah, another one) met us there with his own boat. He had a fourth person with him, not named Jim.

We had difficulty getting the fiberglass boat into the water, as the engine did not pivot up in any normal way due to the way Jim had mounted it.

We had to hand carry it into the water and then quickly hop in, as Jim pulled on the crank to start the engine. I hadn't yet heard the engine and was surprised at how loud it was.

We were sitting perhaps two and a half feet from the engine and the exhaust was blue and oily and following the wind. It was essentially blowing directly into our faces and the rear of the boat was decidedly lower than the front; the engine was really pulling it down.

We were floating though, so Jim opened up the throttle a little to get moving. The other Jim had already put his boat into the water, so he hopped in his and we all began to go downriver.

The wind was picking up as Jim was throttling up and down, trying to find the sweet spot where the boat would trim up out of the water just enough to glide along smoothly.

There was no sweet spot.

Jim throttled up and the boat jumped up out of the river as the prop dug into the water. The boat simply didn't weigh enough for this to function properly.

He quickly settled into a cadence of full throttle, boat jumps out of the water, slams back down with a loud clap against the water's surface only to dig in as tho we were going to swamp it and sink, then full throttle again.

We both got tossed around enormously. I immediately grabbed hold of the tiny (decorative?) windshield that was still attached to the fiberglass shell as it was the only rigid piece of the boat that could be used as a handle.

We began racing the other Jim. This prompted Jim to accelerate the cycle, leading us to fully exit the water at least twice, all while the wind was picking up and the waves on the river were now two or three feet high.

We did this for approximately 20 mins, getting beat up and fully-soaked each time we crashed back down from having leapt out of the water.

It began to rain and the entire situation turned miserable instantly. We turned around and headed back to the boat ramp.

The next time I saw that boat it was on a wooden frame in Jim's back yard. I don't think it was ever in water again.

—

I don't know what lesson the boat episode provides. Sometimes things are just dumb.

Don't do dumb stuff.

A little more seriously, though - inventing stuff is sometimes exactly what has to occur to solve a problem.

When I needed to securely access my client's source code over the internet, I invented hosted source control.
The raw ingredients - the foundational components - already existed. I assembled them along with my newly written application to create the new thing.

This worked because the components were generally aligned with each other, each was properly sized or interconnected correctly already.

The way I'd put them together was new and unique.

This fiberglass boat was the exact opposite. None of the components were meant to be put together.

This fiberglass shell wasn't strong enough to hold an engine, there weren't any proper seats, and the hole in the floor where the paddles used to be had been patched with a home-made sort-of-fiberglass mixture.

Calling this a boat was being charitable.

The point of this is that even though - by definition - the process of invention involves creating something out of nothing, you have to be realistic in your approach.

Otherwise, you'll end up with a 135hp engine bolted to a 9ft fiberglass boat.

A BIG RIG, A HIGHWAY & AN INSTANT DECISION: CRAZY IS AS CRAZY DOES

This is the single-most unbelievable story I tell people.

Couple things:

This is 100% true. There was a third person with us - Tommy G. He was there and saw everything.

Do not ever - under any circumstances - try this. Ever.

We'd been driving around one evening and stopped in at the truck stop to gas up. We encountered Tommy G there and before long, Jim said 'let's go to the east side.'

This was short-hand for 'let's go to the strip clubs'. I wasn't into that, but Jim was. I think he was dating a dancer at that point, in fact.

I reluctantly agreed. Jim must have asked Tommy if he wanted to go, because he hopped into the back seat.

I was driving my Suzuki Samurai. The top was off and the weather was great, maybe 78. It was around 10:30pm as we left the truck stop at Allenton and got onto eastbound 44.

What Jim did next defies rational explanation.

Just east of Eureka, Jim stood up from the passenger seat and climbed over the windshield. He was now crouched on the cowling between the windshield and the hood, holding onto the windshield frame with one hand and motioning to me as he yelled:

"Pull up behind that truck!"

I was traveling at 65mph and now had my best friend on the hood of my vehicle. This was no time to screw up.

You know that saying 'Not my circus, not my monkey'?

Well, this was now my circus and my monkey was on the hood of my truck.

I turned my headlights off as I moved in behind the semi-tractor trailer. It was your typical refrigerated cargo truck, perhaps carrying meats or fruit. Who knows.

I held the speed at exactly 65 while Jim swung around and placed his feet on my front bumper. I couldn't see his feet, of course, but as he began to stand up, that's the only place his feet could have been.

His left hand was behind his body as he arched his back toward the Samurai while waving me forward with his right hand. I was now inches from the back of the semi - the large full-height doors of the trailer were seven feet or so in front of my face. At 65mph.

Jim reached over with his right arm and grabbed hold of the steel lock-bolt that ran all the way up each door and was part of the door lock.

As soon as he had gripped that, he stepped onto the truck's rear bumper and pulled his body in tight. He was off the Samurai and waved me to back off.

As crazy as the situation already was, it became fully insane a second later.

When I was about 30 or so feet behind him and again in the other lane, Jim began to frog-crawl up the doors.

He made it to the top and disappeared.

It was at this moment that I turned to look at Tommy in the back seat. He was speechless.

I followed the semi in the right lane like that for another mile. We approached and went under a bridge and I was expecting to see Jim get knocked off and killed.

This was not a great experience. But I'd been committed to it, so I watched the truck intently.

Approximately half a mile past the bridge, Jim surprised me by poking his head out from in front of the trailer, on the reefer unit[17]. I couldn't see any part of his body so I don't know if he was standing there or sitting on the unit, but I will never in a thousand years forget the huge smile he had on his face as he waved at us.

_____

[17] reefer is trucker slang for refrigeration unit, the system that keeps trailers cold and allows fresh foods to be transported across long distances without spoiling

He then motioned 'up' and 'back' with his finger, pointing to the sky and then to the back of the truck.

He was going to try to get back onto the Samurai.

He disappeared and less than a minute later he reappeared at the back of the trailer, on the edge of the roof. He swung his body over and essentially just slid down the lock poles until his feet were on the semi's rear bumper.

I had already pulled in behind the semi and turned my lights off. I eased up to the bumper as I'd done before.

Jim was now holding on to one rod with his left hand while looking back at me, waving me in to exactly where he wanted my bumper to be. He hard-waved a 'stop' and I held that position.

He turned his body slightly and placed his right foot onto my bumper. He was now partially on the semi and partially on my Samurai. I was laser focused on maintaining my speed and trajectory with absolute precision.

In one fluid motion, he swung his body around so that his left leg was momentarily on nothing, letting go with his left hand at the same time.

His left leg briefly touched my front bumper (it must have though I couldn't see this) as he spun and more or less landed on the hood of the Samurai with both arms out.

He pushed off the bumper and landed toward the back of the hood. As he did this, he grabbed hold of the top of the windshield and hoisted himself over.

That last action left a foot sized dent in my hood.

I was both amazed and pissed.

I yelled at him "Why in the hell did you do that?!"

"I always wanted to try that. I knew you were the only driver who could do it."

We continued on to the east side.

—

Whoever you're with at any given moment:

You're taking on whatever risk they decide to assume as though it's yours.

Because once they commit you to something with life and death stakes, **that risk is yours**.

Choose wisely.

That said, if you do get committed like this - like Jim committed me to his stunt - you better be laser focused on delivering results.

Not every risk you take on will have life and death consequences (hopefully almost none), so this example is clearly way out on the edge of what you'll plausibly encounter.

But the lesson applies just the same: if a particular outcome depends on you doing your part, however small it may be, then ensure you get it done.

Relatedly, if you've willingly taken on the risk, for example by joining a startup as a very early employee, you've made an explicit commitment to manage through the risk to its best outcome, even when circumstances quickly and radically change.

PART III: THE STUNTMAN FANTASY

PRACTICE MAKES PERFECT: FINE-TUNING RISK MANAGEMENT

During my senior year, I'd purchased two motorcycles. The first was a plain old Honda 350 that I used for daily rides to & from work, and the second was a more exotic dirt bike - a Hodaka 125cc Wombat, which was nicknamed the Combat Wombat. I began to spend time practicing my jumps on the Wombat. I got pretty good, too. At my best, I was jumping over 30 vertical feet and approximately 70 lateral feet.

I decided that I really was going to be a stuntman, and I'd specialize in motorcycle jumps. It was spring in my senior year of high school, the weather was fantastic & I was getting plenty of daylight to practice each day after school.

Practice consisted of riding large loops around my parents' four acre property, building up speed for the jump at the end of each run. Their property had a spectacular feature that made this almost too easy - the previous owners, who had built the original house, had begun construction on a detached garage or barn and had dug out a huge hole into the side of the hill adjacent to the house. But they ran out of money or something and quit the garage project soon after, leaving this giant hole that barely had grass growing in it when we moved in.

What this created for me was nothing short of a perfect jump setup. The long, 1/10th mile driveway was all uphill, with a short flat distance across the parking lot (yes, the house had a parking lot) to the hole, whose back end was a dirt wall over 15 feet tall, slightly pitched outward such that it was an intense, natural ramp. With enough speed, I could ride straight up & over. The "over" was my jump.

I got so good at this & the bike felt so natural to me, that when I was riding, I became the bike. The Wombat was super lightweight at 198 lbs and I could throw it around like it was 10 pounds. I'd jump for hours, often crashing and occasionally getting hurt, but I never stopped.

I learned from every jump, making adjustments to my speed, position on the seat and orientation of my feet on the pegs for each subsequent jump. I was getting better and became more convinced I could do this for a living.

I was managing for the risks that I could see - the ones that would kill me if I didn't get right. Go fast enough to do a good jump, get some air & hot-dog a little, but don't go so fast that I fly straight up & crash. As I increased my speed & thus height of my jumps, survivability was a real concern.

I was routinely jumping 70 feet, predicting where I'd land to within inches of where I *did* land. I was managing risk, baby. Or so I thought.

What I didn't have any clue about was how to transition from stuntman wanna-be to real stuntman. I had no connections and very little money saved at that point (I was spending my money on my cars & keeping my bikes running), so my plan, which consisted of me going to Los Angeles & having my bike transported on a truck, fell apart pretty quickly. I made one phone call to a trucking company and decided I couldn't afford to truck my bike to LA.

I recall someone suggesting that I rent a trailer to haul the bike myself, but I didn't have a truck of my own at that point.

I didn't even tell anyone, either. By then, I'd decided against college and had made vague assertions about becoming a stuntman. I didn't let anyone watch me practice, though. I'd learned early on that even though I was a great rider, Jim was brutally critical of my style. It was nuts, because I was a better rider than him. But because he made me self-conscious, I decided to practice alone.

I know my mom & sister watched some of my jumps, as they'd occasionally mention it during dinner. But almost without exception, my riding & jumping was a solo activity.

This allowed me to focus, adjust & get better. It's a behavior that has stuck with me to this day, in fact. I tend to work alone, iterating over stuff many times until I have it right.

But now I had no idea what I was going to do. I had my job at the gas station, which I hadn't yet quit.

TRAINING WITHOUT A PLAN: NOW WHAT?

I got really good at jumping a motorcycle because I practiced for hours a day, but that really wasn't part of any kind of plan. Unless you consider simply getting good at jumping a plan.

It was a single step. The moment that I was faced with the reality of, you know, what's next? of getting the motorcycle out to Los Angeles, which is where I thought I had to be, the stuntman journey ended. I couldn't afford that.

I found out that this would have cost me about $3000. I didn't have that so I didn't pursue it.

That was the end of the stuntman idea, the stuntman fantasy. So now what? I had to figure out what was next.

The lesson that became apparent is that there's got to be a plan. If I'm going to put a lot of time and energy and practice into something in order to become skilled - in order to become good enough to do something else with that skill - there has to be a bigger plan.

I had to be able to measure things, to know I was done with one step so I could move on to the next and then the next and so on.

Until then, it was simply this very abstract idea: to be a stuntman. I was doing tangible, discreet things with the motorcycle with high repetition. I was jumping the motorcycle. I was becoming very good at that. But that was a singular, isolated step. It was almost table stakes, in fact, to becoming a stuntman.

You want me to be a stuntman, you have to be able to do stunts. And my stunts were the motorcycle work, so I was effectively at step zero. Even though I put a lot of work into *becoming* really good at jumps within the context of becoming a stuntman, I hadn't really done any work. There was no plan.

I had to figure out a plan. What's the objective and what are the discreet steps that have to occur in order to accomplish milestone goals that collectively comprise the objective?

I'm kind of bummed that it took me that long to figure that out. But I'm pleased that I did figure it out. Some people still don't understand that. And they're just bumbling through life, letting things happen to them with absolutely no plan and wondering why things don't get better for them.

That's not what I'm doing. In fact, look precisely at what I'm doing right now. I decided that I'm going to work on writing and Tincup Voice full time after I left the last full time gig, as a result of my No Assholes rule.

So I quit that, but I had a plan for what I was gonna do before I quit. And now I'm doing it - I'm writing. I am using Tincup Voice to facilitate writing… I'm writing, and it's part of the objective of publishing a book.

You want to be a writer? You have to write. You want to publish a book, you have write a book.

—

Make a plan and do the stuff in the plan.

It's so obvious when it's said this way. This is a lesson that I trace directly back to the stuntman fantasy.

By the time I reach the planning phase for something new, I've given it quite a lot of thought. I have a good sense of what the final outcome looks like because I always start with a simple question:

What problem am I trying to solve and what does *solved* look like?

Envisioning the end state this way allows to me work backward in my head, decomposing the end-state into discreet things that I need to produce.

One I have that vision, I put it into writing. I like lists, so I'll sketch out the vision in list form.

This makes it really easy to note high-order aspects or features of the new thing while allowing for super-easy addition of detail as it emerges.

Imagine you're creating a log management system. You want to keep costs as low as possible and only utilize compute resources on-demand.

You envision employing a lightweight agent on the local system that communicates to a lambda[18] to process log files. You

---

[18] AWS Lambda, the functions-as-a-service offering that allows developers to deploy single functions to AWS-managed containers without the need to manage the underlying infrastructure. This service is on-demand & costs only for the execution time.

want to make both user experience (UX) as well as the user interface (UI) intuitive, functional & beautiful.

The list format is super powerful. I use it all the time.

This is how I would sketch out that application.

```
Logman

1. Serverless
   1.1.manage dev/deploy cycle in sls
   1.2.decide on stages
   1.3.create a gitlab repo
2. Agent
   2.1.phone home
   2.2.API
   2.3.API key
3. Selectable logfiles
   3.1.system
   3.2.mail
   3.3.httpd
   3.4.other
4. secure / auth
   4.1.expiring token
   4.2.public / private key
   4.3.letsencrypt or aws cert
   4.4.load balancer
   4.5.listeners
   4.6.target group
5. Application
   5.1.node
   5.2.plain javascript
   5.3.what's the payload, if any
6. View by
   6.1.Event type
```

```
6.2.Timestamp
6.3.Pattern match
6.4.Frequency
6.5.Source
7. Search
7.1.string
7.2.regex
7.3.time period
8. UI
8.1.vue components
8.2.colors
8.3.text | icons, both
8.4.font face & size
8.5.highlighting
9. Account
9.1.Free
9.2.Developer
9.3.Pro
```

If you create your list - *your plan* - using a project management tool, you'll have a lot of decoration around these items. They'll be tasks that have work flows, allow comments, attachments & can connect to your source control (assuming the project involves coding).

You can also create a list like this in your phone's Notes app and convert it to a checklist instantly. As you complete tasks in the list, check them off.

This gives you an immediate status of the project with visual cues about what's still to be done.

Some of you reading this may be excellent project managers and caught yourself chuckling at the obviousness of what I just covered.

You're in the minority.

This seemingly simple skill - decomposing a complex project into discrete functional subsystems and then articulating those into trackable tasks - which you then actually track! - is, in my experience, not widely practiced.

It can improve your effectiveness and time management enormously.

This book started out as a list that itself became the Table of Contents. I then wrote the chapters that were listed. And a lot of that writing was actual speech, as I've mentioned.

Remember, in order to do the stuff in the plan, you must first actually have a plan. Put it in writing.

I've talked a lot about risk-taking. Early in my career, I developed the concept of my risk profile: how much risk I could and would accept along various dimensions such as salary or revenue, personal safety, health, housing and transportation.

It's easy to think about an aggregate risk profile this way:

I'll accept near-zero risk with regard to my transportation, because I can afford to purchase or lease new vehicles and keep them maintained. This ensures that they're always in top condition & reliably available whenever needed.

I accept quite a bit of personal safety risk every time I ride the motorcycle. But I use a professional quality helmet, an armored leather jacket, kevlar-lined & ballistic nylon padded jeans, steel-knuckled racing gloves and steel-toed riding shoes.

The gear provides impact, slide and entanglement protection. This can be a tough topic to discuss, considering that the equipment is meant to prevent serious injury or death. But it's a part of my risk profile that I deal with every time I get on the bike.

The Icon jeans have a kevlar mesh sewn into the interior of each leg and covers the entirety of my seat. Each leg also has a 14" removable ballistic nylon pad as well as a manufactured-on 3/4" thick, 5" round exterior rubber knee pad.

Kevlar provides a layer of skin protection that can withstand a tremendous amount of friction. If I come off the bike at speed and begin sliding, the exterior denim of the jeans will burn off rapidly as I slide down the pavement. That layer of Kevlar gives me a few more moments to expend the kinetic energy of the slide - to slow down and stop sliding - before it too tears & burns off, exposing my skin directly to the pavement.

Massive skin injuries don't immediately kill motorcyclists, but it's a huge factor in post-accident infections that can & do kill riders. Even a low-speed accident that results in road rash can put a person out of commission for weeks or months.

It's like having third degree burns.

The jacket has removable ballistic nylon pads at the shoulders and elbows and is constructed with an extra layer of leather in the back center.

This provides impact protection along nearly 15" of each arm & back. Slide protection is provided by the full-grain leather of the jacket's exterior. The jacket can be hot - the day that I rode across the desert, the temperature was 108F. To remove the jacket - to be cooler - on a day like that would require me to have no protection on half of my body. That's a solid No every time.

My choice of steel-toed riding shoes rather than boots surprises non-riders when they see them.

"Why aren't you wearing boots? You'll break your ankle if you fall off."

No. The amount of energy involved if I come off the bike will be an order of magnitude or more greater than simply '...tripping & falling'.

I wear low-cut steel-toed heavy leather shoes with 2" rubber soles for two reasons:

At low speed, the steel toes & leather provide both impact & slide protection. At higher speeds, the low cut means that my ankle remains a natural twist or break point.

Recall above where I mention entanglement protection? If I leave the bike at speed and my foot catches on something stationary, like a street sign or guardrail, a low cut shoe may simply get pulled off my foot.

My ankle may also break & spin around. At worst, the shoe gets stuck on the object long enough to tear my foot off. The break point is at my ankle. I don't lose a leg.

Say what?

If I'm wearing a boot that is cinched up over my ankle and is tight against my calf, that thing isn't going to come off when it catches on that sign or guardrail. My kinetic energy still has to go somewhere though, so my leg may get torn off at the knee - the next major break point - as I continue sliding down the road.

Good thing I didn't break my ankle.

The helmet's role is obvious. Ditto for the gloves. I do not today ride without either.

If I leave the motorcycle saddle during a ride, the probability of me surviving is higher than if I hadn't geared-up. The risk profile is constantly in play.

We have some savings, so I'm willing to accept some risk around new revenue or salary. I burned the ships[19] to write this book, so that speaks for itself.

Health is an area where I employ a mixed approach. I accept almost no risk with regard to my skin now, as I've had multiple skin cancers. I get my prostate checked at the recommended frequency, too. I walk daily and have been losing or maintaining a goal weight for several months. Beyond that, I don't get too concerned.

You get the idea.

Collectively, this is my risk profile. Thinking about it this way helps me make decisions that are scoped to a specific area, being careful not to take on new risk in one area that also raises my risk profile in another.

—

If you don't identify and **manage your risk profile**, you can be **overwhelmed** & experience a **cascading failure** when even a minor exogenous change is introduced.

---

[19] 'burned the ships' means you're fully committed to the new task or adventure. There's no turning back to old habits or old ways. You have no ship so there's no way back.

PART IV: CORPORATE LIFE TO ENTREPRENEUR: FLIPPING THE SWITCH

ST. LOUIS TO DENVER

I worked at progressively more interesting and better-paying jobs in St. Louis from 1981 - 1990.

In 1990, I was working at Monsanto - wearing a suit, starched white button down shirt and tie every day - as an IT analyst through their coop student[20] program connected to Washington University or UMSL. I attended both but don't recall the program's affiliation.

I'd been a coop student for three terms, receiving an exemption for two extra terms due to my role. I supported PC hardware in the corporate offices & was well-liked.

But I ultimately was not allowed yet another coop term, and was laid off along with some others in a larger staff-reduction event. I was out of work.

The timing on this was awful - two other big companies had layoffs at the same time. St. Louis was in a down-turn.

I found an IT job at an insurance company in Denver & moved out there in May '90.

---

[20] Co-op or co-operative education is a method of combining classroom instruction with work experience

I bought a Honda CBR1000 Hurricane in 1992. It was used but had very low mileage and a unique custom paint job.

Fashion choices and the general lack of protective gear aside, I usually wore a helmet. The photo below was taken after I'd ridden from DEN back to STL for a visit in July.

The Hurricane was my seventh bike and was by far the fastest. It had a 998cc (60.9ci) liquid-cooled 4-stroke 16 valve DOHC inline-four cylinder engine with a published top speed of 160mph.

It put out 135 hp at 9250 rpm; it was, in practice, a street-legal race motorcycle. I had Michelins[21] on the bike when I owned it and quickly learned the value of those incredibly rounded sidewall profiles:

The tires gripped the pavement like clamps when dipping low to the pavement at high speeds around curves.

I learned to ride fast and hang off on this bike.

The Hurricane was my daily ride for nearly two years. As I was riding it everywhere, I began to inject my risk-taking style into virtually every ride. I'd speed and hang-off nearly 100% of the time I was on the bike.

I wish I hadn't done that. When I see riders - usually young, usually male - riding like that, I wince. I know I rode the same way, but it upsets me.

It's too easy for a speeding bike to be missed in a car driver's mirror and get hit. It's too easy for any one of a hundred things to go wrong and result in the rider getting killed.

I regret riding that way, even briefly, but I know why I did it: the adrenaline rush. The Hurricane could deliver my adrenaline fix in seconds. It felt great.

That feeling of speed - of the pavement, ground and the world - rushing past you as you propel forward at over a hundred miles per hour is hard to explain to someone who hasn't ridden.

---

21 Michelin Tires, well known for producing racing tires

And so I sought out opportunities to go even faster. To my credit, I didn't ride fast in traffic or anywhere near people walking.

Out riding on the west end of Morrison Road one afternoon, the conditions were perfect: dry, sunny day, perfect pavement and virtually no traffic.

I opened up the Hurricane and quickly picked up speed. The bike felt great. Super smooth, still accelerating, but at a slower rate. I hit 130mph and continued.

From 130 to 135 took a couple seconds. Reaching 140 took a few more. I could see that I was running out of clear road soon, so I held the throttle.

I hit 145mph. This was the fastest I'd ridden and would remain the only time I rode that fast until the return ride from St. Louis.

On that return trip, I'd lost a couple hours waiting out severe weather in Columbia, Missouri. I was trying to make up time as I crossed the Kansas - Colorado state line at 145mph.

My risk-taking was still very present, but I was developing a sort of code: no one but me could be put in jeopardy when I rode fast. My moral code and ethics - my integrity - was emerging in how I rode.

I was on the edge with that bike but was also very grounded. It's a dichotomy that shows up frequently.

I moved from the insurance company IT job to a network support job at a large telecommunications company in 1993. That was a technically interesting job that introduced me to the internet as it was emerging.

I wrote one of the first - perhaps *the first* - web sites in the company that was used to do real business work: it delivered packaged software updates to the branch desktop images. It was pretty cool considering how crude the available tools were.

I learned HTML and a ton about routing. While that job was not at all personally satisfying, it was critical to my early development of essential internet-centric skills.

It didn't last long, though. I was laid off along with a few thousand others in the summer of 1995.

But this time was different. I didn't want another corporate job. Work for somebody else - often a jerk - and be subject to layoffs again? No thanks.

I was going to work for myself.

WORKING FOR YOURSELF: HOW "RUSH" & MOTIVATION ARE INTERTWINED

Within a couple weeks of that layoff, I was consulting on a data migration project in Chicago. This was a forgettable project in most respects beyond the most important: it was the first of many.

The gig proved I could charge a high rate for a specific project, get paid and move on. This was a model I employed for a couple more gigs before randomly landing on a project that involved setting up the source control and builds[22] for a small software company in Boulder.

I realized something critical on that project: the software developers hated dealing with both source control as well as building the application.

This was true across many companies. I rapidly developed expertise in designing and implementing source control and build & release management systems. This was very lucrative.

Companies were desperate to gain control over their software development process and build their applications in a repeatable way.

Techniques I developed would become the central components of my first real company. I'd raise capital, hire developers of my own and produce a product.

---

[22] Build refers both to packaging software into an application, "building", as well the output of that packaging, "the build"

From that first build & release project going forward, I took on only software configuration management gigs. I became very, very good at implementing source control, build & release systems and advising on development practices.

It took a little while to gain a critical insight - I could make a whole lot more money by taking projects outside Denver.

The Denver market was just too conservative. There was some software development occurring, but not enough to create a competitive market for talent. It also wasn't sophisticated enough yet to highly value the specialized expertise I had in software configuration management.

Starting in late 1998, I only accepted projects outside Denver. I generated a lot of revenue.

In the spring of 1999, I was working yet another build system contract for a company outside Boston. This project was pretty frustrating, as the internal company developers were neither particularly skilled nor motivated to solve problems.

They would stay in their narrow areas of responsibility and not deviate outside to learn new things or solve bigger problems. I encountered many, many issues on that project as a direct result of this behavior.

One of the more maddening issues was that I had to be onsite at the company location in order to gain access to the source code, which was necessary to test any build system work. This may seem reasonable, but it was a huge constraint. I was effectively unable to do any work outside the six or so hours per day that someone was available onsite to physically give me network access.

I was thinking about ways to solve this problem as I fell asleep in the top-floor bedroom of the 200 year old farmhouse where I was staying, when I sat straight up in bed and almost yelled to no one but myself:

Freepository

"Source code repositories would be freely, but securely, available over the internet. You would authenticate over the internet and be able to commit changes right inside your browser."

Immediately upon my return to Denver I began work on creating the new company that would produce Freepository.

In the fall of 1999, I was working a contract for a software company in Sausalito. During the time leading up to this, I'd created the company and produced an early functional source code hosting service, Freepository.

I'd made some money from consulting and capitalized the company with both cash and the service itself for a total personal investment of $200 thousand dollars.

I began hiring and raising operating capital. The vision & scope of what we were building was bold.

A full software development environment in your browser: source control, bug tracking, build & release management, all accessible securely over the internet from anywhere in the world

In January 2000, I met some investors at a demo day at Fort Mason in San Francisco. They immediately committed to my full round.

I'd raised $700 thousand dollars and had 16 employees when I secured a term sheet for an A round investment of $4 million dollars. This was scheduled to close in May of 2000 in New York City. Several high net worth individuals were participating and had already committed capital.

We had a full page ad in one of the many glossy internet-centric magazines that seemed to be everywhere.

ConfigMan was hot shit.

There was $1.4 million dollars in the escrow account that was being used to hold these commitments.

Everything looked great and during one of my visits to New York prior to the closing, I had my own driver for a couple days.

Things were moving very quickly. Until they stopped.

There was a particularly brutal day in the markets and the losses were enormous. The people who were expected to wire capital that week didn't. The entire remainder of the round - $2.6 million dollars - vaporized.

This was an exogenous event but it ended the company. There was no Plan B for this, effectively a meteor-killing-the-dinosaurs type of black swan occurrence.

I spent the next two weeks with increasing urgency calling everyone I knew - and dozens of people I didn't know at all - looking for an infusion of capital.

The answer was loud and consistent: some variation of 'I can't right now with the markets being crazy'.

I knew that my plan couldn't be implemented with only $1.4 million without significant changes and certainly less hiring. We wouldn't have the service completed soon enough to cover our burn rate - $140 thousand per month - with sales. There was nothing to sell yet.

I made the incredibly difficult decision to send it back. Technically, the cash would have gone into a legal limbo where the investors - with near certainty - would have sued me and the company for a return.

I opted out of that. It was **over**.

This was really hard to do, but it was the right thing. The vast number of unknowns at that point meant taking the smaller amount of money would have been morally wrong.

Everything I'd planned for and promised my team depended on being able to fund the full plan. I couldn't in good faith try to pretend that I'd just figure out a new path - I wasn't sure we'd be able to adjust like that.

Laying off my own team over the next three weeks was the most difficult professional task I've ever done. I gave everyone one last paycheck and made a decision around that that personally cost me $46 thousand dollars.

We'd used a payroll service - recall, we had a headcount of 16 - and as a result, we had payroll taxes in our own escrow account.

I authorized the use of that cash to ensure that my team's last payroll was as close to full as possible. That was technically illegal and the IRS kicked my ass with a $46 thousand dollar fine.

It may have been illegal, but it was the right thing to do.

–

There were a lot of lessons from ConfigMan. These are the most important.

Hire smart, not fast.

A variation of this rule has been popularized by others, but this version is critical: don't hire anyone who isn't smarter, more highly skilled or experienced, or have more domain knowledge than you.

I made one critical 'lower' hire and this person hired a few B players. I had already resolved this when the capital markets crashed; it had nothing to do with the investment collapsing, but it was a huge time and energy sink during the period I was negotiating the closing.

That person also hired two consultants before we had any projects onto which to place them. Part of my plan was to jump-start sales of the product, the dev-environment-as-a-service (called an ASP back then), using the early consulting customers to both partly fund ongoing development as well as be beta customers for the service when it emerged.

We had two highly paid consultants on the bench for nearly three months. They billed zero. My exec in charge of the consultants - that critical bad hire - had a lot of excuses for not getting them deployed and billing.

I was newly attacking this issue when the market crashed and the investment failed. It suddenly made no difference.

Don't spend money you don't have.

"It's going to be wired to your account in eight days."

Eight days. That's less time than it takes for a beer left out in the sun in your back yard to go skunk. It's less time than you allow yourself to schedule a flight and purchase airline tickets.

I transitioned from holding a negotiated-terms equity investment for $4 million dollars with a closing date eight days out to the end of the company in less than four hours.

That eight days went from seeming like a few minutes to the end of time. It would never be reached, so it had all meaning and yet no meaning.

Had I not spent the "…money that was coming" before it was actually in the bank, we may have survived. That's a huge *if*, obviously, as enterprise software entered a nuclear winter later that year with regard to corporate spending.

But the $60 thousand I spent on an in-house data center and the $45 thousand in consulting headcount wages were instantly valueless. That $105 thousand would have provided another month's runway to obtain funding.

This was a huge tactical error that I will never make again.

Violating your ethics in desperation is still a violation of your ethics. Don't. Ever.

This is embarrassing to discuss, but I own it.

One of the calls I made after the investment tanked was to the CEO of a competitor that had emerged. During a previous call he'd initiated, he expressed interest in buying my company.

"Are you still interested?"

That led to a conference call with his CTO and a senior engineer, which I arranged from my phone in Denver.

We spoke and it was cordial but non-committal on their part. As we ended the call, I inadvertently didn't hang up. I'd been using speakerphone and the call was still open.

The receiver was back in the cradle, but a second or two later I heard one of them say 'are you still there?' and before I could respond, the CTO replied 'yes'.

They didn't realize I was still on the line, even though I had setup the conference call. They began to dissect the earlier conversation and in a moment of desperation, I stayed on and listened.

They spoke for less than a minute and hung up. I was immediately struck with a sense of shame and guilt, not having any way to explain to myself what I'd just done. It was a breach of trust and my personal ethics like I'd never done before (or since).

I quickly called the CTO back and through a halting voice told him what I'd just done. He thanked me for admitting to it and said something like "...I know some CEOs who would do that any chance they got".

For the record, it was clear from their conversation that they weren't interested in pursuing an acquisition. My actions didn't change the outcome, but the lesson stuck with me.

PART V: ENTREPRENEURIAL RISK-TAKING AFTER A FAILURE

THAT SUCKED: PICK UP, DUST OFF, AND DO IT AGAIN

After ConfigMan failed, I had to quickly generate revenue to restore financial health to my household. That episode had been a huge time and cash loss for me, and the household now had no income.

I created another company through which to take on consulting projects, keeping it separate and distinct from the earlier company.

One of my last acts as CEO of the earlier company was to release the source code of Freepository under an open source license. I knew that I wanted to continue working on it, but couldn't legally or ethically if it remained the private IP of the company that was about to be dissolved.

I put it on Sourceforge, which had emerged a few months after ConfigMan. It was downloaded many times & I subsequently received support requests from 3rd parties. People were using it.

I also trademarked the name Freepository. This gave me rights to use the term I'd invented if I chose to at some point in the future offer the service again.

I moved the data center into my house and after a brief period of being offline, put Freepository back online.

Friends who've heard me talk about having a data center in my house? This was it. It was loud.

That data center gear wasn't mine, so I didn't keep it for long. I sold it (at a loss - no one wanted expensive gear at that time) and used the proceeds to pay some remaining ConfigMan legal bills.

I purchased new servers of my own and migrated the service to them.

It was surprisingly easy and fast to pick up new projects. Even with all the uncertainty in the enterprise software market - as well as the broader financial markets - many companies were still spending money on existing initiatives.

I secured many lucrative projects over the next several years, earning large sums. I was on a plane a lot. It was during this period that I picked up the majority of the almost one million air miles that friends have heard me mention.

Freepository was gaining a lot of new members and I'd added a couple paid plans. The service was healthy but my primary revenue came from the consulting projects.

As earlier stated, this was really lucrative. I could do a couple projects and then take a little time off, as the revenue was so good.

My family and I began taking multiple nice vacations per year. We remodeled our kitchen and purchased a full compliment of motorcycles, gear and a high-end trailer for weekend family riding.

The consulting was going really well and more than once I considered hiring another engineer to take on some of these projects under my consulting company umbrella.

Staffing firms make huge profits from managing the billings of its consultants, so this model was proven.

I just could never bring myself to hire someone though and subject them to the same risks that I'd forced my earlier employees to assume.

I didn't want to have to lay anyone off again. As a result, I became significantly more cautious in that regard. I would do nothing that required employing someone else.

This made it nearly impossible during that period to consider creating another startup in any meaningful way.

In early 2001, I'd taken on a contract role at an emerging software company in San Francisco, Wily, that resulted in an offer of full-time employment at the end of the project.

I accepted that and stayed for a little over a year, moving on yet again to another very lucrative consulting project for a major financial services company headquartered in San Francisco.

I enjoyed my work at Wily but decided that I didn't want to simply work for someone else again.

Thus began a series of projects at walmart.com, StubHub, Macromedia, Juniper, Oracle and Lab 126 that were ... you guessed it... lucrative, but not terribly personally satisfying.

I was very good at what I did, but I was essentially solving the same problems over and over again. The challenge was no longer there.

My approach was safe and paid well, but it didn't excite me. I had to shake free of the FUD that I'd created in my head around starting another company and the risk-taking it required.

It took me a few years to fully internalize that I wasn't going to be happy just doing these build and release consulting projects over & over again. It didn't help that they paid so well.

That inertia was in conflict with my overwhelming and increasing desire to take on more risk.

I skydived for my birthday. I rode my CRF230 solo on the track a lot, pushing my jumps well beyond what my then-current skill level was. I was crashing routinely.

During my last attempt to do a real jump, I setup a long ride around the base of the camelback by the pond out at the motocross racetrack in Watkins, Colorado. I'd done this hundreds of times but had always played it safe and pulled off a 10 or 15 foot jump. Respectable, but not challenging.

That day I was gonna let it rip and see how far I could go. Mentally, I was back on the Combat Wombat and ready to jump 70 feet.

I jumped somewhere between 25 - 30 feet and crashed bad. My front tire landed hard at a 40 to 50 degree angle to my direction of travel and caused the rear of the bike to cartwheel.

I was thrown up and over the front of the bike as it slammed into the ground next to my body. Had I not been wearing a full-face helmet, I would have had serious, life-threatening injuries.

My chin guard dug into the dirt and carved a 2" gouge in the ground. My thumb snapped back and broke as I flew over the handlebars and it got stuck between the brake fluid reservoir and throttle.

My entire left arm was raw from landing on that side and skidding out to a stop on it. My left knee had a deep, heavily bleeding gash in it from having caught it - I think - on the clutch lever that was broken off. As far as I can tell, my leg broke the clutch lever as I flipped over and then my knee was stabbed by the broken stub.

I limped back to my truck with the bike and met up with a friend who had driven out to ride with me. Instead of riding, we told stories about riding, which sometimes is better.

My thumb was still in a brace when I saw Wily friends at the hotel in San Francisco a few days later. It got some laughs when I said "…I almost couldn't go skydiving on Saturday because of that wreck."

I didn't ride that bike much at Watkins after that, deciding that my jumping days were behind me. I did become pretty good at riding wheelies, though.

I rode a wheelie approximately 200 feet in a grass pasture while camping at my wife's cousin's property.

I sold those bikes a few years later and have almost exclusively ridden only street bikes since.

Fear will control everything you do if you let it. Conversely, it will control what you *don't* do.

You're afraid of failing so you don't start the company.

You're afraid of a "No" so you don't pitch the VC.

You're afraid of being responsible for someone else's paycheck, so you don't hire anyone.

Fear will kick your ass and steal opportunity from you in a hundred subtle ways every day. I've found that honestly acknowledging my fears is the only way I overcome them.

This doesn't always work, but it usually does. I'm still reluctant to try a jump again - that fear is real and is very convincing.

But other fears, like "I'm afraid no one will read or like my book, so I'm not going to write it"? Screw that.

Don't let fear control you like that. This was an epiphany for me.

Like I say earlier, make a plan and then do the stuff in the plan. You can be cautious, but you have to stop listening to the FUD[23].

---

23 FUD - Fear, Uncertainty and Doubt. FUD is often used in sleazy marketing to cast doubt on competitors or in political campaigns to smear opponents. Internal FUD is self-doubt, the impostor syndrome, that inner voice that says you can't do something

Some fears are healthy. They keep us alive by helping us avoid situations that will actually kill us. Pitching a VC and getting rejected isn't going to kill you.

Think of it this way - you already have the No because you didn't even pitch her. You already have an unsuccessful company because you didn't create it.

Etc.

Let's get real for a moment. Many - most? - fears are centered on rejection and our desire to avoid it. I don't want to be rejected. It sucks.

When I was young, rejection avoidance was the driver behind not asking out certain young women. I feared rejection, so to avoid it, I wouldn't allow the opportunity for it to even occur.

In hindsight, this was ridiculous and self-defeating. But so many people behave this way that it's worthwhile to explore it.

There is an obvious but overlooked way to handle rejection. Acknowledge to yourself that the condition or situation that represents the rejection is *already your current state.*

The outcome that you want - the investment, the company that does [x], or a relationship with another person - can only be obtained by taking that risk.

Risk the rejection.

It's the only path between you and that outcome. There aren't any shortcuts and it may be difficult emotionally, psychologically and even physically. There is simply no substitute for it.

Take the risk.

You just might get a Yes. You already have the No.

After nearly losing everything to the failure of my first company, I was reluctant to take on additional risks, as I described in the previous chapter.

Cutting through all the individual reasons for my doing specific things, the entirety of my conduct during this time can be summed up as wanting to remain in control. Of everything.

Of course, this was impossible. As the maturity of software development tools improved, there emerged easily obtainable in-market substitutes for my bespoke consulting, in the form of new open source applications.

Need a build system that is free, somewhat easy to use (I'm being generous here), and mostly well-documented?

Hudson (which became Jenkins after the fork)

Need free hosted source control but don't want to deal with the nightmares (you've heard horror stories) of either CVS or Subversion (SVN) [24]?

GitHub, Bitbucket and later GitLab

This was especially ironic because I'd invented hosted source control. At its peak, Freepository was hosting 3 billion lines of code for 400 thousand developers globally. But almost no one

---

[24] CVS and Subversion were popular source control tools. They were open source, free to use and thus implemented at many large corporations instead of commercial tools.

wanted to use SVN any more and my attempts to layer in a git offering fell flat.

I began to instead focus on repository conversions and migrations. Companies that had been using CVS for years were now struggling under the constraints that it forced:

TAGGING OPERATIONS[25] WOULD TAKE HOURS

THE FILE-TREE-BASED REPO STRUCTURE WAS EASILY DAMAGED

AND FRANKLY, IT WAS STILL PRETTY BUGGY

Migrating from CVS to SVN became a new specialty that was also pretty rare in the market. As a result, I could - and did - charge hefty fees for this.

In one particular project that friends have heard me discuss, I billed $80 thousand dollars for three days of work.

Now, to be fair - that $80 thousand was paid out over 50 days, but the problem that the company needed to solve - migrating from CVS to SVN in under 15 days of clock time - I'd solved in the first 10 minutes of the initial call scoping out the project.

---

[25] Tagging refers to applying a label to a set of source code revisions. Every time a build occurs, the involved revisions are tagged so that the build can be reproduced by referring to the tag. This is critical in order to produce and apply bug fixes.

Using my newly invented technique, their CVS repo[26] - the one holding the core OS[27] of every single piece of networking gear this company produced for its global customer base - could be migrated, with history, in under 37 hours. That's a weekend.

Collapsing that initial 15 days of clock time, which was the best the company's internal team had been able to produce, unblocked a major corporate initiative that had come down from the CEO:

"Speed up our ability to release products ASAP."

As long as that CVS tagging operation took more than 8 hours and locked the entire repo while it was occurring, there could only be one build per night.

And if that build broke? Forget it. You're looking at a multi-day delay that required more builds and tagging operations.

I spent the rest of the three days modeling the automation and proving the solution. Everything after that was other people coordinating and scheduling the rest of the migration.

The $80 thousand was cheap vis-a-vis the ongoing cost of the problem.

---

[26] Repo, repository. This is the collection of source code files and all their revisions in a scheme that allows the developer to manage the evolution of software.

[27] Operating System. These are software rules & instructions that control how a computer functions, for example how to open, save and store files. A network device OS controls how network traffic is categorized, prioritized, and routed between network segments.

I had traded control of the hosted source control market for creation and control of the repository migration market.

This lasted a good three years before the opportunity was essentially exhausted. Companies still looking to solve this problem that long into CVS' life were opting to just export the source without history and introduce it as-is into SVN. No small share of companies were also completely skipping SVN and going directly to git.

SVN became the source control tool no one wanted to use almost overnight. Certainly nothing new was being put into SVN.

Freepository membership and usage plateaued in 2010 and never recovered. I ran it for another six years because the teams that *were* using it depended on it heavily.

But by mid-2015, the data was clear: even long-time members were no longer active and years of positive growth had been replaced by negative churn.

In one last act of control, I shut it down in May 2016.

KEEPING YOUR SENSE OF HUMOR

I've had a dry sense of humor since I was a kid. Sarcasm, irony and absurd situational constructs are my standard conversational elements.

When ConfigMan failed, my stress level was extreme. I'm sure I was a jerk (unintentionally, but still) to everyone around me at least once.

In hindsight, it's obvious why I behaved like an ass in situations that reached some trivial level of inconvenience or hassle - I could no longer use my sense of humor to defuse my own stress. Things just weren't funny right then.

This was a critical insight that took a while to grasp, but it allowed me to regain a large part of who I was and to become a better person.

For context, at the beginning of my extensive air travel period, I was in a paradoxical situation: making a lot of money on the current project, but still dealing with the emotional and financial fallout from ConfigMan's failure.

I was abusive one day to the car rental counter person at SFO. The issue was ridiculous - some minor thing wasn't quite right - but I gave him a ration of shit that was completely disproportionate to the problem.

I regretted my behavior immediately and as I exited the rental car garage that morning, I went over and over - and over again - in my head why I'd reacted that way.

In the abstract, it was clear that I still didn't feel in control of my situation. Where I *could* exert some control, as in the rental car exchange, I did so.

But there wasn't any balance, no equilibrium, in these situations. The imbalance was extreme, in fact, and not only did I end up feeling like shit afterward, I'm certain that the person on the receiving end of my shit sandwich didn't feel very good either.

I decided that I wasn't going to behave that way again. The best trick I had at my disposable was my sense of humor. I began making jokes not only to - but also *with* - the people with whom I interacted daily.

This helped me deescalate the stress of traveling, of which I was doing a ton. I have to imagine that the people around me preferred the jokes to the nastiness.

Over the years that I travelled in and out of SFO, I rented cars from that same man more than 200 times. We became friends and would discuss family vacations, health and dozens of other routine topics like friends do.

A few years after that first bad interaction, I mentioned to him how awful I'd felt after it and that it had prompted me to reflect. I'd decided that day to do better.

His reply has stuck with me all these years later:

"You were an asshole to me. The next time I saw you, I expected that again. But you were different and I was glad.

I now look forward to seeing you."

A sense of humor. Use it.

I found that after my first startup failed, I was less interested in maintaining my older pre-startup friendships. My interests were now significantly more aligned with technology, business and how to create something new.

There was almost no overlap between that and the interests & experiences shared with my pre-startup friends.

I first noticed this during my time at Wily. Wily was still technically a startup when I joined (I became employee #23 if I recall correctly), even though they had just signed the company-making contract with IBM.

I was a part of a seven person engineering team and the first hire whose role was purely infrastructural - I wasn't developing the core application, but rather the build & release tools. I was also responsible for the source code repository.

We were a small team each making an out-sized contribution to the success of the company. At twenty-three, the small size ensured that everyone involved was a risk-taker.

I was in my element.

The friendships I made at Wily almost 20 years ago remain some of my best. Though I don't see everyone nearly as often as I'd like, five of my engineering teammates have visited me here in Denver.

To a person, they all went on beyond Wily to other startups, with a few of them starting their own. I attended an early company formation dinner where the name was chosen for one of these startups; I provided the source control for them. That company was later acquired by Yahoo for $300 million.

I'd see these friends with high frequency even after I left Wily. Much of my consulting work was in San Francisco and I was essentially commuting between DEN and SFO.

We'd meet for dinner or drinks at least monthly. This kept me current on what they were doing, which often involved long conversations about technology, funding or marketing.

These conversations were intellectual fodder for my risk-taking predisposition. My desire to remain immersed in the startup ecosystem was fully fed by being in San Francisco, often around this group of friends, every week.

This is a bit of a self-reinforcing feedback loop. If I'd not been looking for San Francisco projects after ConfigMan, I wouldn't have connected with Wily nor would I have made all those friends.

And of course, I left Wily to take on another San Francisco-based project. I stayed at Schwab for thirteen months working on several projects.

I made new friends at Schwab as well, but none were entrepreneurs. They were all employees. I don't think it's a coincidence that I didn't maintain friendships with any of them.

FRIENDS FEED THE NEED, PART DEUX

In 2008, I began attending a series of conferences in Denver that focused on technology, startups and deep-thinker topics like freaking sharks with lasers... almost.

I met and befriended a lot of people at these early conferences who remain close friends today. Some of them (hey there) reviewed the draft of this book pre-publication.

I need to back up a bit and mention that in 2006, I did try to raise capital again for Freepository. Among many others, I had meetings with two Denver area VC firms and the results were mixed.

As I maintained when I started Freepository in May 1999 and raised capital that next January, hosted source control was going to be a billion-dollar (at least) market.

I was executing a technical road-map for Freepository that included facilitating secure, remote command line access to the service.

This meant that I had to figure how to make pserver[28] secure as well as run for tens of thousands of repositories on the same hardware. Among CVS' many constraints, its network-access daemon protocol, pserver, was plaintext. It was insecure. And the CVS daemon by default ran on one port only - there could only be one CVS repository serviced by one daemon per hardware server.

---

[28] pserver was the service daemon that facilitated cvs usage across a network. It allowed normal users to login to cvs through a password file unrelated to the system itself

That didn't scale at all.

I could easily present an SSL[29]-secured web view of a member's repositories because of the use of back-end processing to generate maps of authenticated users to resources.

I needed this same security, mapping and isolation from the command line.

So I implemented secure command-line interaction, bypassing the web site completely. This was a fantastic enabler for members of the service, as it allowed for Freepository to be used in build systems and other automation that didn't (yet) connect using web APIs.

I integrated something called sserver, which was the pserver, or password server daemon that allowed CVS to use password-authenticated user sessions across the local network, with SSL compiled into it.

This meant that connections could be made across the wire using the same protocol as encrypted traffic bound for an internet banking or e-commerce site. It couldn't be sniffed for passwords or source code content.

That 'local network' piece wouldn't ever work with a URL, of course. That's where the true genius (hey) of the sserver implementation came into play:

---

[29] Secure Socket Layer - the communication protocol that encrypts traffic as it traverses the network. Banks and e-commerce sites use this to prevent traffic snooping

Every repo got its own server port. Every single member who had a top-level project had a unique, silo'd, fully addressable CVSROOT[30] that was reachable across the internet using the protocol:user@server:port notation that CVS already supported.

I had to implement a functional change in xinetd[31] in order to make this work. The core xinetd supported only 1016 active services (the system file descriptor[32] (FD) limit was 1024, but xinetd used several FDs internally), as a means to preempt resource exhaustion with respect to open file handles.

Freepository needed to support more than 1016 CVS repository services by orders of magnitude. I made a change to the source that allowed xinetd to fire up the maximum number of FDs possible within the OS, without regard to system resources.

My hypothesis was that if the server running Freepository was sufficiently robust, i.e. fast CPU and a shit-tonne of RAM, then it should be able to handle opening up as many ports as I had compiled-in file descriptors.

It worked.

This meant that Freepository instantly supported as many secure, silo'd repositories - each with a fully manageable

---

[30] CVSROOT is a variable that defined the repository location and how to access it

[31] xinetd - Extended Internet Service Daemon, is a super-daemon that manages internet-based connectivity. It is/was more secure than the earlier inetd.

[32] File descriptor is a mechanism the operating system uses to manage resource utilization across the system. They're essentially handles, or labels, for complex processes

password map - as were numbers of services that could be spun up in my customized xinetd.

When I exhausted the number of available ports on one server, I could simply add traffic to another. The use of the server name in the CVSROOT variable meant that I had effectively no upper bound to the number of repositories the service could now support. I could simply add another server to the system and map to it in the member's admin panel:

```
sserver:joe@fp1.freepository.com:3001/fp1/repo_a

sserver:sue@fp1.freepository.com:3002/fp1/repo_b
.
.
.
sserver:jesse@fp2.freepository.com:5019/fp2/repo_c

sserver:sarah@fp2.freepository.com:5020/fp2/repo_d
```

This led to a significant increase in Freepository membership. Fully 100% of traffic in and out of the service was secure, something that the handful of other services that had emerged had not yet figured out how to do.

I had opened up the CVS command line to secure use across the internet using Freepository's own command line client. I provided the source to that so anyone could inspect it - and see *exactly* what it was doing - and compile it themselves.

So as I began raising capital again in 2006, Freepository had just over 10 thousand members working in ~4000 active projects. It was clear that the service was actively being used by teams as evidenced by the number of members who were active in each repository. This wasn't just a bunch of random single-person projects.

NASA had a couple projects on Freepository, as did multiple governmental agencies. One country's treasury department had multiple projects that - though I never inspected them, I could see the project names as they were created - appeared to be managing critical aspects of... financial stuff.

It was wild how many well-known companies just showed up and started using Freepository. I'm certain that having secure command line access was a huge facilitator in that, as the amount of build system traffic that I saw after that went through the roof.

Build traffic was so immense that it occasionally acted as a DOS[33] attack against the service. That was fun.

Early proof of that billion-dollar market vision was becoming visible. I needed to reach more potential members and decided to sponsor those conferences.

The sponsorships (first hosted dinners for attendees and later vendor booths for my other services) were between $1.5 - $5 thousand dollars, so this wasn't a big spend by any means. This was a calculated risk that, if it worked, would prime the pump and start the Freepository flywheel spinning.

---

[33] Denial of Service - a high number of simultaneous connection attempts by one or more remote computers, for example all to a company's web home page, in an effort to exhaust resources on that company's web server, thus denying service to other legitimate users

But it didn't generate any net new business. This was unexpected, so I discontinued sponsorships after a few years.

I was too early, of course, but the vision I had back in those early days - the vision that prompted more than a few VCs to ask me "a billion dollar market? Are you sure?" - played out in the market as I'd predicted.

Back to those two Denver VCs - the first was initially very interested, but then when that 'partner' (the son) discussed the deal with another 'partner' (his dad), the conversation ended.

The dad didn't understand how or why anyone would ever put source code on someone else's server. I wished I had known prior to spending any time with the son that he didn't have any decision-making authority.

That objection was exactly - almost word for word - the argument that one of the co-founders of Sun made to me when I pitched him in San Francisco in 2000.

The other VC firm was less ambiguous. As I explained that some long-time members had said that Freepository changed their lives (direct quote), one of the partners sort of snickered and just walked out.

I was stunned. The remaining partner was left to try to explain that action (he couldn't) and finally said that in order for this (me) to be taken seriously, I'd have to quit the consulting. I'd have to burn the ships.

This was after the service already had more than 10 thousand members. It was a weird interaction, but fast forward to 2008 and I'd become friends with both of those VCs after they left that firm and formed a new partnership.

So I now had a new set of friends with similar technology interests, many of whom were startup founders themselves. They understood the adrenalin rush of starting something - going from nothing but an idea to something that tens of thousands or more people - were using.

I also became friends with the conference organizer and helped run some sessions and panels. One of the early panels that I facilitated included the CEO of a now publicly traded company during *his* pitch time period.

Anyway, my new peer group was a perfect fit. I could - and did - frequently discuss ideas with them, occasionally taking their advice, but more often just synthesizing their input into my own plans.

"It's just data."

I heard this a few times during this period and I internalized it. Everyone has an opinion but no one but you knows what's right *for you*.

I continued to learn, explore and experiment with new ideas with the expectation that I'd ultimately discover another great idea and take it further than Freepository.

I began using AWS while I ran Freepository and knew first-hand the cost-savings it represented versus co-location at a local physical data center.

For context, I had contracted with a local data center co-location provider in DEN to rack my servers. Freepository members in Australia & New Zealand had been experiencing latency accessing the service, so I needed to get directly onto a POP[34] to eliminate as much of this latency as possible.

My contract, which I signed two months before AWS S3 was announced, was structured such that I paid a variable rate for actual bandwidth. This seemed reasonable in theory, but in practice, it got out of hand quickly.

During one of the last months I used the co-location service, my invoice for bandwidth alone was $3 thousand higher than the month before. I couldn't correlate this to any changes - new members or repositories - and so disputed it with the data center provider.

They didn't budge on the charges, stating '...whatever caused the increase, was out of our hands'. I had next to no visibility into this and was furious that I had to simply trust this vendor.

I paid the overage and vowed that the second my contract's term expired, I would never again use a co-location service.

---

[34] Point of Presence, a direct interconnect to an internet carrier. POPS form the backbone of the internet.

The lesson there is perhaps less meaningful than it could be, as today you have the option to pay-as-you-go with AWS, Azure, Google Compute Cloud or even DigitalOcean. But still - make sure you understand the outlier cases you're accepting when you sign multi-year contracts with service providers.

I started two more services during this period around solutions to what I saw as big problem spaces, but ultimately were niche or unscalable, i.e. non-investable:

BUILDS AS A SERVICE
LEGACY SERVER MIGRATIONS AS A SERVICE

To anyone who just read that and asks 'what about lift and shift vendors? that seems like a big market.'

It's lucrative but incredibly niche. The CAC[35] is very high, which constrains the players to a small subset of either well-funded startups that are willing to burn a lot of money to acquire a single customer or existing large companies that layer migrations into current offerings.

It is also a naturally shrinking market. Every migration that occurs reduces the size of the overall market. Virtually no new systems or applications are being developed for on-premise-only implementation. New work is going straight to cloud infrastructure like AWS or Azure.

---

[35] Customer Acquisition Cost - dollar cost that a company spends to acquire a customer. High CAC is bad unless there is a correspondingly high Lifetime Value (LV) for each customer

Legacy stuff is a finite market. It isn't growing, so you can't scale a solution to meet demand. Demand will naturally always be contracting.

Urgency to migrate may increase, thus increasing the value of *specific* migrations. But even that exhausts over a finite time period and you really have nothing more than a repeat of the earlier repository migration scenario I'd experienced. Lucrative, bespoke, finite.

I pitched over 40 VCs during this period. About a third were immediate 'No's, which are actually fine, another third were unresponsive - not even a quick 'No', and the last third were substantial, high-quality interactions that involved multiple calls, demos and partner meetings.

Each of the two new services used AWS infrastructure and cost me (effectively) pennies to run. It was fun and allowed me to continue living in the startup world. I had compelling, elegant, rock solid technical solutions to these problems.

I'd built services that I could demo. I could credibly get meetings with VCs and discuss all aspects of the problem I was solving, the market size and the value I saw in my solution. Getting someone excited about these problems, though, for the reasons mentioned above, was a non-starter.

I made a lot of VC friends through this process but obtained no term sheets. It's hard to come away from that not feeling pretty deflated. But I kept going, because I like creating things and I knew that eventually I'll hit the right combo of large-market opportunity and solution.

By maintaining these friendships, I was satiating my own need to be an entrepreneur. Even though I wasn't risking *everything* like I had 15 years earlier, I was out there. I was doing it.

My need to take risks and get that adrenaline rush could be filled by writing software and all the activities associated with pitching my ideas to friends and VCs.

ALL MY FRIENDS ARE VCS. HOW'D THAT HAPPEN?

Surrounding myself with entrepreneurs, investors and academics in the startup ecosystem naturally constrained my peer group. This resulted in the creation of many new friendships with founders, VCs, academics and technology industry analysts & reporters.

An interesting dynamic that evolved is the number of VCs who became friends. A disproportionate number of my closer friends - i.e. we communicate routinely outside of any deal context, we socialize etc - are investors.

This has been both good and bad. I deeply value my friends, to be sure, but this can - and surely has - create[d] a signaling issue [36] when I've tried to raise capital.

Let me address the 'try' right here: at least one of my well-known VC friends maintains the dictum that there is no 'trying to raise' - you either are or are not raising.

It makes for a nice sound bite that expresses the need to fully commit to a raise, but it misses the reality that every entrepreneur faces:

UNTIL YOU GET A CHECK, ANY ACTION IS *TRYING TO RAISE.*

That's privately grated on me for some time. Anyway, I have tried to raise several times, including a couple times with friends.

---

[36] signaling issue refers to one VC interpreting another VC's deal interest as a positive or negative indication about the quality of the opportunity or the entrepreneur

I have a friend who is now a VC at a top-tier firm in San Francisco. He and I worked together at Wily and became close friends. He's visited me at my home in Denver, he's sought my advice a few times over the years at key decision points, etc. The stuff friends do.

During his term at Harvard Business School, Dan asked me to write a short paper describing an experience I'd had with him "… at his best". I chose to write about the evening that he & his cofounders, along with one other ex-Wily friend, had named his new startup.

This is the company formation dinner that I previously mentioned, but that isn't the part of the story I told. We were at Cha Cha Cha's in the Haight, enjoying some drinks, chips & salsa before our dinner was served.

I choked on a chip.

I went to the restroom and tried to dislodge the chip myself but failed. I was getting light-headed and desperate and hurried back to the table.

I grabbed Dan and motioned rapidly at my throat. He quickly understand what was happening and performed the Heimlich Maneuver. The chip popped out and we resumed our dinner.

So he and I have a connection.

He's heard some of the Jim stories I've recounted and as a result, thinks those attributes - the wildness, the craziness - is a core part of me. Even though I was never as wild as Jim, that's impossible to provably assert today.

As a result, he says he won't invest in me for two reasons: he doesn't ever want to be in a position to have to fire me because we're such good friends, and - this is the one that bugs me - because I'm 'nuts'.

That's a tough one to refute. Maybe he's joking, but he's said it twice. There's not much to say to that beyond, 'ummm... no, but I respect that you don't want to invest in a close friend.'

I've initiated contact with other VCs who I either didn't know at all or only marginally knew, perhaps via twitter interactions, and once it's clear that I live in Denver, this question is frequently asked:

"Do you know the guys at [x] VC firm?"

"Yeah, they're good friends"

"Oh, cool. Are they participating?"

"Umm, no."

That's happened a few times and it's really awkward. Having VCs as friends is definitely a dual-edged sword kind of thing.

PART VI: THE ENTREPRENEUR AS FAMILY MAN

VULNERABILITY IS A STRENGTH

That's counterintuitive and reads like a line from a fortune cookie. Let me explain.

It's an insight I had at about the same time I was struggling with career decisions, specifically around whether to join another traditional company.

The consulting had gone from lucrative and easy-to-find to almost impossible to source in under 18 months. I'd also decided that to be more supportive of my family, I needed to travel a whole lot less. This was after having spent much of the prior 10 - 11 yrs traveling nearly full-time during the business week.

I had to face the reality that I may have to take on a regular job again. That felt like admitting failure.

I finally decided that this wasn't a failure but a show of strength. I was putting my family first by allowing myself to take a job in Denver.

I swallowed my pride and took the job. I felt extremely vulnerable professionally - my identity was that of an entrepreneur, heavily tied to working for myself, on projects of my choosing, when I wanted, where I wanted.

All of that was now set aside. I would no longer have those same freedoms, at least for eight hours each day. But here's where a funny thing happened - after the initial embarrassment eased, I felt really good about this choice.

I was home every night. My commute was under ten miles, not the 965 miles that I'd faced each week the entire previous decade.

And I constructed a reality that allowed me to work from home every day. The way that occurred was completely unplanned, but it played out pretty well. I've always been much more productive when working solo, so this model was a natural fit to my work style.

I wasn't chasing contracts or getting up at 3:15am every Tuesday to go hop on a plane. A paycheck kept showing up in my bank account.

Allowing myself to be vulnerable - to consider and then accept the 'regular' job - made me a better parent and husband. It made me stronger.

That lasted six years before I had to enforce The Rule.

RISK-TAKING NOW INVOLVES OTHERS

Captain Obvious just called with an important message: as soon as you marry, buy a house & start having kids, your risk profile changes.

You now have to consider how your actions impact the rest of your family... your finances... time at home, etc.

I had already been consulting for a little over a year when my first son was born. I'd briefly taken a regular job just before my second son was born, but soon after went back to consulting and then began the ConfigMan journey.

My wife and both boys were accustomed to me traveling. For the first several years of their lives, I wasn't around for two - three days each week. I tried to make up for this by doing fun stuff on weekends, but I know that wasn't a completely fair trade.

The boys didn't choose for me to travel. Arguably, neither did my wife, Jen. But consulting was bringing in a pretty decent income and the projects were primarily in San Francisco.

A lot of my income went into the house and some toys, as I've mentioned previously. We had a ton of fun on our motorcycle adventures; each of us had our own bike and we'd trailer them somewhere in Colorado for the day or a weekend and have fun camping and riding.

But when it came time to take on bigger risks, like starting another company and investing a lot of my own capital... I was very risk-averse. I couldn't - *wouldn't* - take on that level of risk again when Blair & Brandon were this young and Jen wasn't working outside the home.

As the boys grew, the consulting opportunities became fewer and farther apart. As mentioned earlier, I took on a regular job in Denver as a result.

This was after a lengthy discussion with my wife during which we weighed - honestly and openly - the risks I was forcing on the rest of the family by continuing to consult.

The gigs were good and occasionally very good, such as the $80 thousand dollar migration project. But those were becoming deviations from the norm as opposed to the typical contract as had been the case early on in my consulting.

As I type this, both boys are seniors in their respective universities. Jen has her own job that she enjoys. We spent nearly 10 thousand dollars on a replacement air conditioner and furnace a couple weeks ago when the original equipment stopped working.

We have some savings. The lawn looks great.

Things are pretty normal, almost boring.

This was a factor in my leaving that last regular job. I can now resume my risk-taking without jeopardizing the needs or comfort of anyone else in the family.

Don't get me wrong - money gives you freedom. I've experienced a few points in my life when I didn't have enough. It sucks.

Optionality is what people want, even though almost no one outside the startup world calls it that.

You can create optionality for yourself with one of these four fundamental currencies:

Money

Time

Skill

Knowledge

Money is obvious - you can, within reason, buy the outcome you want. Want to live on the ocean with the beach literally steps from your back door?

Buy a property that provides that. It will be expensive, but with enough money, that's an option.

Time is a little less obvious as a currency, but no less valuable. With enough time, cet. par., you can accomplish almost anything. "I want to write a book". Cool, give yourself three - six months to do just that - and only that - and you'll have a book at the end.

You've traded the opportunity to do other things with that time for the specific outcome you wanted.

Skill is also obvious and easily understood. If you've put in the time (see above) to learn a skill - and you're good at it, fast or whatever the measure of 'expert' is in that skill - you can trade use of your skill for money. You then use that money to create additional optionality. Rinse & repeat.

Knowledge as a means of creating optionality is similar to skill, but it's more abstract. It's part of the multi-sided market that I've told my boys about since they were young.

You trade money and time for knowledge, creating optionality for yourself that typically results in you being able to trade skill (*practiced* knowledge) for money at some future point in time.

Interdependencies between these four currencies play out in repeating cycles across your life. Understanding what your tradeoffs are in any given transaction can help you avoid situations where you aren't creating optionality for yourself.

But treating money alone as a measure of your personal value is foolish. I've seen a lot of entrepreneurs and VCs - not friends, but people I've encountered up close - accept this as part of their personal values.

It's pretty gross to see. I want enough money to make my own decisions, be my own boss and not have to deal with assholes. I don't need a billion dollars. I come back to that point in the next chapter.

Banking the less tangible stuff, like experiences & college degrees, is a far better use of time & money. We traveled a lot when the boys were young; they had their own passports almost before they could walk or talk.

Over the course of a few years, we traveled to a particular resort complex south of Playa del Carmen, Mexico 10 or 11 times. We swam, rode ATVs through the jungle, toured cenotes and enjoyed some Vegas-quality live entertainment shows.

We went to Europe, once with the boys and once without. Jen and I spent a long weekend in New York City.

We also camped a bit and after we got the motorcycles, we'd ride out at Rampart Range or the Watkins track somewhat frequently.

As soon as the boys graduate, they'll have banked an important asset of their own: the college degree. That'll give them both choices they wouldn't otherwise have as they begin their own lives fully outside our home. They'll have optionality at the beginning of their adult lives.

You know what else is more important than money?

Integrity.

One of the lucrative contracts I had was in early 2004 at a major bank in Salt Lake City. This was one of the very few projects I took that wasn't in San Francisco.

The project manager on that contract was, I found out later, significantly late and over-budget on the delivery of the contracted results. The bank was pressuring him - apparently even threatening legal action - to deliver or get kicked out.

That's what I walked into, having no idea of course about those details.

One day a few weeks into the contract, that PM began acting oddly. He'd ask about things I'd said at a meeting that occurred when I wasn't even in Salt Lake City.

Later, he suggested that I was responsible for contract language that been written and executed over a year before I arrived. It was inexplicable behavior.

The next or perhaps second day after that, the entire office was startled by the PM yelling - loudly and aggressively - at another team member. This wasn't horsing around - it was angry, threatening language.

The yelling had gotten my attention so I was looking straight at him down the corridor between cubes when he violently threw a pen at the person at whom he was screaming.

I decided at that moment 'enough'. I discussed this with Jen and the next day gave the PM notice that I would not be returning after that week. This was a two-day notice.

I couldn't - and more importantly wouldn't - continue in an environment like that. The person being yelled at became really quiet and withdrawn for the remainder of the two days I was there.

By staying, I would have been endorsing that PM's conduct. So I left. That decision cost me about $100 thousand in billings.

I would make the same decision again tomorrow.

I'd been itching to get a road bike - a highway motorcycle - almost since I sold the Hurricane. My personal favorite for a while prior to buying one was the Indian Chief Classic.

I bought the bike you see on the cover in August 2015 and began riding it daily until the weather forced me to park it.

This bike felt and rode unlike any I'd had to that point. Its engine is nearly twice the displacement of the Hurricane and it has a completely different stance.

The Indian is a cruiser. It's designed to go as fast as you want while looking as cool as possible. Both the name and the bike's lines are an homage to the 1947 Indian Chief - the valanced fenders are a unique Indian design element that's unmistakable, even from a distance.

I began experimenting with speed on the bike.

There are a few roads relatively close by that have that needed mix of good pavement, great visibility and low traffic required to ride at speed without endangering anyone else.

This felt familiar but in a new way. I was now 20 years older than when I last rode the Hurricane, but as I opened up the throttle, everything just clicked.

I could ride fast and get a pretty good adrenaline rush without risking anyone's safety but my own. But I geared up - every time, and still do. I mentioned that when I discussed my risk profile earlier.

I'd allowed increases to my risk profile with regard to the high speed while simultaneously decreasing my risk profile with all the gear.

This was a perfectly rational calculus to me.

That next spring, I rode out to San Francisco to see some friends. The ride was a little sketchy on the first day - the wind was awful in western Colorado and it continued to beat me up as I rode into Utah.

I considered turning around and going home. I talked about this with both my wife and a friend who is also a rider - they both encouraged me to sleep on the decision and reevaluate in the morning.

I stayed at a hotel in Green River, Utah after getting off the highway really early. After a decent dinner and a good night's sleep, I decided to continue.

I'm glad I did.

The rest of the ride was amazing. The cover photo comes from that trip - I took it on my phone on the side of Highway 50 somewhere near Hinckley, Utah.

The solitude on that trip afforded me a lot of time to think - and rethink - how much risk I was willing to take on and what tradeoffs I was willing to make to remove some of my daily stressors.

I wanted to be happy again with what I was doing and what I was working on every day. That happiness had been gone since early on in the regular job. The brief honeymoon period I'd had with it was long-since over.

I decided to work for myself again on that trip. It took a while to implement the plan, but I did have one. Ultimately, the timing of my change was driven as much by my own desires as the actions of others.

More on that in the next chapter.

That riding friend I mentioned earlier? He and I decided to ride part of the Colorado Backcountry Discovery Route on adventure bikes.

Adventures bikes are street legal enduro style motorcycles, a cross between a classic dirt bike, a street bike and a scrambler. They still had big engines - 1200cc - and were somewhat heavy, but they typically have knobby dirt-style tires that are suitable for highway use and high clearance.

They are designed to be ridden on the street as well as off-road in the dirt & gravel.

My friend (hey Rob) had purchased one of his own and had ridden it for a couple years, I think, when we began planning this.

I rented one just like his and he rode down from his home in Toronto. By the time he reached me, he'd already ridden further than we'd planned to ride together.

Overall, the ride was a blast. We hit a lot of long gravel roads that I'd never seen before and I've lived in Colorado for nearly 30 years. It was amazing.

But there were also a couple points where our riding styles - and risk profiles - diverged. Rob was a lot more comfortable on his bike, as should be expected, since he'd ridden it for a couple years. He rode faster and was able to throw it around a bit on the dirt and gravel.

I had all of 8 hours riding time on my rental before we first went off-road.

I hit some slick mud on a somewhat steep incline at the beginning of Corkscrew Pass and dropped my bike. This was both embarrassing and problematic - Rob was riding ahead of me and didn't immediately realize I'd crashed.

I had a minor injury on my leg (a giant bruise) and busted up the rental bike a bit ($750 in repairs upon my return).

After several minutes, Rob returned to find me roping off the bike to pull it back upright. I was still thinking that I'd just get past this section and be fine.

That's when a guy appeared on the trail, riding downhill in a Razor buggy, telling us that "...this trail isn't for you".

I wish that it hadn't, but this got inside my head. I decided that I didn't need more serious injuries or damage to the bike, and so I told Rob that I was turning around.

This sucked. I know he wanted to ride up over that pass. I did too. But I had to decide in the moment to adjust my risk profile down.

The rest of the trip was great, but I sensed that Rob was now doubting my riding ability. That bugged me a bit, but it was fair. He'd ridden all the way from Toronto to do these off-road sections and was intent on riding them.

In that panoramic photo above, we're on a long gravel road near Cathedral, Colorado that stretches for close to a hundred miles, connecting numerous ranches and smaller homesteads. It traverses across several large expanses of open range and in one section hugs the river, with the occasional meandering through stands of Ponderosa pine.

It was breathtakingly beautiful. But it was gravel, mostly loose, of a consistency that made higher speed riding for me really challenging. As soon as I'd speed up a bit, my rear wheel would lose traction, putting me on the knife's edge of losing control.

I wasn't having fun with the gravel, so at the end of that 30 or so miles where the gravel road intersected with Highway 50, I opted out of any more.

Against my better judgement, we split up on two sections. Rob rode the dirt and gravel while I stuck to the highways, even though one of the 'highways' I chose turned out to be a 30 mile gravel road itself.

For the first solo ride, we decided we'd meet up in Buena Vista for lunch. I'd take Highway 50 up and around through Poncha Springs and Rob would ride up over Old Monarch Pass.

That worked well and we had a nice lunch at a pizza place in Buena Vista. Being able to depend on texting each other locations and ETAs made this super easy.

The second time we split up was after we'd spent the night in Avon. The next morning, Rob wanted to try an old logging road that he'd found on the map that (in theory) connected into Kremmling.

We decided to meet for lunch in Kremmling. I'd take the highway and Rob would take that logging road. He'd have to ride west a bit on Highway 70 to connect to it, but that didn't seem like a big deal.

I was less than halfway to Kremmling when I hit that unexpected gravel road. I really wasn't into it, but tried to make the best of it.

The vistas through there were stunning. I saw a sow bear and two cubs run across the road less than 75 feet in front of me - it was amazing.

Ironically, Rob dropped his bike on the logging road when he was riding solo. He got upright but hurt his back in the process.

He'd texted me his GPS coordinates and let me know what was happening. I knew where he was and if needed, could scramble some help. He's been on a lot of solo road trips and didn't need babysitting, but I'll admit that I was concerned for him.

After a while, he texted me that he'd made it back to Highway 70 and that he'd meet me in Steamboat.

He'd made his own decisions about his risk profile and it wasn't my place to tell him how to ride.

I finished the coffee I was having at the place in Kremmling and headed north to Steamboat.

I was happy to see him when he arrived in Steamboat Springs. We had a great afternoon and evening, filled with a good meal, a few drinks and some long conversation in the pool at the place we'd rented at the last minute.

 The next morning, I headed back to Denver and he proceeded north to the Grand Tetons. He took some particularly gorgeous photos on that part of his ride, too.

That was an amazing road trip that really clarified for me that I'm primarily a street rider now. When faced with the very real, very in-your-face risk of dropping the rental bike more than a few times on the gravel (plus the actual crash in the mud), I chose to adjust my risk profile down rather than up.

Acknowledging that after going into this ride thinking that my off-road skills were are as sharp - or enjoyable - as had been the case years ago was sobering. I won't say I was bragging about my dirt skills prior to this trip, but it was close.

I need to speak to one more aspect of my risk profile with regard to my riding.

Okay, so I've said I like to ride fast. There's a long straight stretch of Highway 105 south of Denver that is perfect for this. In that section, you can see for miles in almost all directions.

Importantly, you can see straight ahead for perhaps nearly three miles. There aren't any intersections, driveways, homes or anything.

There's just the road.

It was here that I first busted out the triples on the Chief. That's my reference to riding over a hundred miles per hour. I can see everything on the road ahead of me, so there's unambiguously no chance to hurt anyone else if I crash.

I may hurt myself, obviously, but that's part of my risk profile. I've accepted that. This was how I would ride the bike - I'm willing to take on as much risk as my risk profile allows, but never - ever - force risk onto the others around me.

On the return from San Francisco, as I rode across the Nevada and Utah desert, I busted out the triples a few times. There were sections of highway where I didn't see another vehicle for more than 50 miles.

Though I'd ridden the Hurricane at 145mph a couple times, the fastest I've hit on the Chief is 120mph. That's the speed at which I begin to float off the saddle... which is kinda freaky. My risk profile kicks in and I ease back off the throttle.

It's really clarifying. I do some of my best thinking - seriously - while out on the bike. I've experienced a physiological connection between high adrenaline jolts to my brain and improved intellectual output.

I don't recommend fast moto riding to anyone. But it works for me. Find what turns on your own creativity and experiment with it.

PART VII: WHAT'S NEXT?

TEACH YOUR KIDS TO GO FOR IT

As mentioned previously, both boys are, as of this writing, university seniors. Jen and I instilled in them the need for and value of a college education since both were young enough to understand the concept.

Like any parent, I've made hundreds of mistakes over the years. I think I did pretty well on the important stuff, though.

Both of my boys are smart. All parents say that, sure, but there's objective validation here: they both got accepted into colleges and programs with very high standards: it's hard to get in.

The acceptance rates at many public universities are 85% or higher. There's nothing wrong with that, of course, but that's not my point.

My sons' schools have nearly identical acceptance rates of 40% and 40.4%. My boys are smart, thanks to their mother.

This afforded them some options. My youngest son got into the habit of soliciting my advice on career choices before my oldest did, but they both do now.

My advice to them has always been some variant of:

Be honest.

Show your integrity in everything you do.

Your **character is revealed when no one's watching**.

Accept and **learn from your mistakes**.

Do what you love.

Do your absolute best.

Don't ever sabotage your **peers.**

Stand on your own. Let your **work speak for itself.**

Work hard now to **create optionality** for your future.

Are any of these particularly earth-shattering in their insight? Perhaps not, but they're not simply platitudes either.

Kids need to hear real advice early and often enough to internalize it. I'd much rather learn from someone I trust providing me actionable guidance than waste time, effort and money before reaching that same conclusion, i.e. learning the lesson, myself.

That's the reason I've bought & read so many entrepreneurship books by other entrepreneurs. They've done the thing I'm doing now & are more likely to have specific advice that is relevant to what I'm doing right now.

Just a few days ago, I cold-emailed someone I'd only known from Twitter asking advice about how they self-published their recent book. His reply was super helpful & will undoubtedly save me a tremendous amount of time & money as I navigate the process. Thanks, Mike M!

(if you're reading this book, the process worked)

At the time I'm writing this, Mike Isaac's book about Uber's tumultuous history was just released. This is an extraordinarily deeply reported story that includes vivid scenes of Travis Kalanick, Uber's founder and former CEO, acting like a complete asshole.

I had the pleasure of meeting Mike for breakfast when I was in San Francisco and am delighted to see him emerging as one of the most important technology reporters of this era.

I won't go too deep into Mike's work here - go buy his book - but instead want to focus on the bad conduct.

Kalanick behaved like an asshole because that's what he learned. It's clear he didn't internalize anything vaguely like the advice I give my own sons. In fact, you could plausibly argue that he actively worked against the moral compass of a fair, decent, rules-respecting individual.

The outcome speaks for itself. He's monetarily rich but the entire world knows that he became rich at the expense of virtually everyone he encountered.

When an investor who stands to make billions from your company compares you to a world-destroying blob of alien slime, you've reached a new low.

He displayed little or no integrity in, well... anything.

What an abysmal way to go through life.

I've been a risk-taker since 3rd grade. While I've explored how my risk profile developed and evolved over the years, the constancy of it remained.

A recent example involves Amazon Web Services, AWS. I first used AWS services in 2006 and progressively utilized more, learning quite a bit about the various services until finally becoming certified as an AWS Solution Architect in 2018.

I decided to take a risk and work for AWS.

I began the process with AWS. I progressed through multiple technical phone interviews and was invited onsite to interview in person.

By that time, I'd been an entrepreneur for nearly 20 years but for reason(s) they didn't share, I didn't get an offer.

I'm confident that my solo work style had at least some impact on this - that I may have been too independent to become an "…AWS drone" (a friend's description, which I think is amusing). My wife says "…they wanted a sheep".

It's interesting to me that two people close to me interpreted the process that way. I didn't see it quite that way, but since AWS doesn't share feedback on the decision process, it's ultimately a guess.

On the day of the interview, I was sporting a Mohawk and wore jeans with my steel-toed riding shoes. I spoke with the confidence of someone who knows what the hell he's talking about. This can be intimidating.

One of the people interviewing me asked how I'd handle a situation if I'd over-committed and then not delivered a promised outcome.

My reply - to each of the four times (yes, four!) he asked the question was "...I try really hard not to over-commit, so that's something that I don't typically face".

I think that the interviewer had a blind spot. He was taking as a given that over-commitment just happens and can't be proactively avoided.

My perspective, from 20 years of creating & managing some really complex projects by myself, is that you can avoid stuff like that by managing against it up front.

Let me give you an example.

In one of my early projects, the client asked me to help perform technical due diligence on a company they were considering acquiring. They needed to know if the technology was real or just smoke & mirrors.

We were to meet in Boston, Cambridge in fact, one winter day. It had been cold, but that day's forecast was to be *really* cold. Like 20 degrees below zero cold.

It was so cold that virtually everything was impacted.

But I'd made a commitment to be there at 8am that Monday morning. So I traveled the day before (duh), but critically, I got a hotel very near the Cambridge office.

I knew that there was snow and bitter cold in the forecast and there might be a problem getting a taxi the next morning.

I wanted to ensure that I could walk to the office, if necessary, in time for the meeting. I printed out a map with the directions between my hotel and the office before I left Denver, in fact.

And so I was there before 8am, even as nearly half the team I was meeting were either late or no-shows.

I kept my commitment because I was careful not to allow it to *become* an over-commitment. This is not hard to do if you are intentional about it.

Anyway, the individual with whom I'd begun the AWS interview admitted to me that the entire process made candidates feel like cattle. It was weird, for sure.

I was upset about the interview outcome for less than 24 hours. What I learned from that experience - with all sincerity - is to not give two shits what others think of you.

If you're true to yourself and unwilling to compromise, you've won.

Another important example occurred very recently.

I left that regular job when I enforced The Rule.

I have frequently said that I have a No Assholes rule, which means I refuse to deal with assholes. I will go out of my way to not be around them. I further state that this rule is strictly enforced.

Three months ago, this company underwent a reorganization in which many people left, many were juggled into new teams and a handful were put in charge of new teams.

This created a situation where I had to interact with an asshole multiple times per day. I joked with my wife that this guy (he's a man) had a personality defect that made it impossible for him to be nice.

The jokes quickly lost their humor when I realized that this person was like this all the time. He berated others on phone calls, spoke ill of any work that had occurred prior to him being involved - referring to the company's handling of issues as "...a shit show" - and he wanted to micro-manage everything.

He was a bully. And this was every day.

He was so oblivious to his own behavior that on a call one day, he recounted a discussion he'd had with his own wife in which she declared to him that "...you don't motivate people with carrots, you use a stick".

Dude, your own wife knows you're a bully.

I finally just said *enough*. My rule was either real or it wasn't.

I learned that my moral compass - my integrity - couldn't abide this conduct. I learned that I still had the same sense of duty to myself - the unwillingness to compromise my principles - as I'd had back in Salt Lake City in 2004.

I resigned.

No assholes, strictly enforced.

WRITE A BOOK, HE SAID RECURSIVELY AS HE STARED AT THE SCREEN...|

I've been writing this book in my head for quite a while. I had a title, some chapter topics and had even committed some text to paper.

But I wasn't really writing because honestly, I didn't much like typing. T - y - p - i - n - g. Do not like. Not a fan.

I wanted to be able to write by speaking. While I'm out walking, while I'm working out, while I'm riding the motorcycle... that's why I created Tincup Voice.

I'm not going to turn this chapter into a pitch for Tincup Voice, but it's important to note that I created it for myself.

I expected others to want to use it, but I was the target customer.

My personal ethics wouldn't allow me to create a classic device-API-dependent iPhone app, one that has access to your contacts and can silently use your microphone, so I implemented the entire service as a web app.

Privacy is important to me, even if I was the only one who ever used it.

I learned how to use the web browser audio API, which allows you to request access to and use the microphone to record speech through a web page.

I learned about the transcribe service, how to implement lambda, a ton about node.js development (I thought I already knew a lot) and of course how to parse a transcription and create a well-formed, editable post.

All from simply speaking into your phone.

My blog jbminn.com is an integration between Tincup Voice and the site. Most of what appears there started off as me speaking into my phone. I'm definitely scratching my own itch.

Anyway, having Tincup Voice available as a writing tool made this a lot easier to start. Multiple chapters started as Tincup Voice posts. The No Assholes section in the previous chapter was produced entirely in Tincup Voice.

As it turns out, I'm hand-typing this right now. So while I began the process heavily reliant on Tincup Voice, I'm wrapping it up using the keyboard.

Writing this book has helped me identify the source of my risk-taking, how it evolved and what effect it had on my character.

Entrepreneurship was practically a foregone conclusion for me. Given my personality type, it was a perfect match. I could take on as much risk as possible, with big rewards if things didn't go sideways.

While I've had neither a billion dollar exit nor is my name as well-known as some other startup founders, I've never compromised my integrity to accomplish what I did.

I'm giving myself a pass for those few occasions early on when I *was* a jerk and *did* violate my personal ethics because I immediately course-corrected.

Those behaviors weren't compatible with the type of person I want to be - the type of person that *I am*. So I quit behaving that way.

That's cost me money.

That's cost me opportunity.

But I wouldn't trade being a person of integrity - someone who is trusted because they're actually trustworthy - for those other outcomes.

I don't want to be another rich asshole.

So what's the bottom line? What are my parting words?

Never stop learning.

Decide on something you want to learn and then do it. Go to Udemy or a similar site & search on that subject. Select a couple high-rated courses and take them.

Put your headphones on and immerse yourself in the videos. Do the exercises. Stop and look things up if you need to understand something better.

I've taken at least 500 hours of video instruction like this. Leverage the fact that you have access to the world's experts literally at your fingertips, for the price of a couple fast food meals.

If video courses aren't your thing, read. Take a class at your recreation center or library.

Volunteer at the hospital - you will learn a ton about how much goes into the day-to-day operations of running a hospital beyond the obvious health care aspects, and you'll be making your community better at the same time.

Block out at least four hours per month to do this - more if you can - to learn.

Never stop taking risks.

I'm not talking about motorcycles or climbing onto semis here. I'm talking about risking the rejection. Put yourself out there. Be vulnerable.

Almost nothing worth having in your life comes to you without taking a risk. This can be really hard to do, especially if you're accustomed to avoiding confrontation, resisting situations where you may feel judged or will get rejected.

If you're surrounded by people who are themselves afraid of taking risks, this will be extra difficult for you. You need to break free of the FUD and allow yourself the opportunity to try something that, yes, may fail.

But it *might not* fail. It might actually succeed. You won't know if you don't try.

Remember that you already have the No. Internalize this and act on it. Take the risk.

Imagine me standing in front of you waving you on and saying

"Go for it!"

Do what you say you're gonna do.

You know how many people consistently don't do what they say they're gonna do?

A lot.

A guy cancels meetings at the last minute. Frequently.

A woman promises to meet her friend at the gym and is a no-show. Frequently.

I'm sure you can think of a few examples of your own that happened just this week.

This axiom developed long ago for a reason:

"You'll know who your true friends are when they show up on moving day."

Be the true friend. Be dependable. You'll be enriching your own life as well as those of the people lucky enough to have you as a friend.

"I'll pick up the moving truck & coffee. See you at 7am."

And finally -

Never compromise your principles.

If your principles - your moral compass - can't survive an encounter with a real-world difficult decision, then they weren't actually your principles & you don't have the ethics you advertise.

Is that a harsh thing for me to say at the end of this book?

Yes.

But this is me saying to your face what you will say to yourself if you compromise your principles for some stupid, short-term gain.

What you let others see is a glimpse of how you see yourself.

Trustworthy. Or not.

Dependable. Or not.

Does the right thing. Or not.

It means you'll have to say no to things that seem like a great idea at the time, to actions that are easier in the moment. The easy way is almost never the right way in those situations and you know it.

If your inner voice - the one that you know is always right - says 'this is sketchy' - then don't do it. The world doesn't need another asshole with a broken moral compass.

Your integrity - the external reflection of your character as expressed by your observable conduct - should be consistent across your adult life.

Your integrity should be like bedrock - firm, unbreakable and foundational to everything you do.

Once cracked, it's nearly impossible to repair.

— jbminn

COLOPHON

Created and published by John Minnihan in Denver, Colorado

Software

Layout & Design:	Apple Pages
Tables:	Apple Numbers
Voice Transcription:	Tincup Voice
Image Editing:	Apple Preview

Typography

Body Text:	Avenir Next 12pt

Hardware

Layout:	Apple iMac
Photography:	Apple iPhone

Motorcycles

Indian Chief Classic	2016 1811cc V2
Honda Hurricane	1987 998cc
Hodaka Wombat	1973 125cc Combat Model 95
Penton Six Day	1974 125cc
Various others	

INDEX